NEGOTIATING
YOUR WAY
THROUGH KOREA

NEGOTIATING YOUR WAY THROUGH KOREA

Richard Saccone

HOLLYM
Elizabeth, NJ·Seoul

Negotiating Your Way through Korea

First published in 2001
by Hollym International Corp.
18 Donald Place, Elizabeth, New Jersey 07208, USA
Phone (908)353-1655   Fax (908)353-0255
http://www.hollym.com

Published simultaneously in Korea
by Hollym Corporation; Publishers
13-13 Kwanchol-dong, Chongno-gu, Seoul 110-111, Korea
Phone (02)735-7551~4   Fax (02)730-5149, 8192
http://www.hollym.co.kr

ISBN : 1-56591-158- ×   (hardcover)
ISBN : 1-56591-162- 8   (softcover)
Library of Congress Catalog Card Number : 00-106351

Printed in Korea

Preface

O ver the years I have heard the complaints of business persons and government officials concerning negotiating in Korea. Most are frustrated dealing in an environment so different from their own. Others have little negotiating experience even in their native culture and are further frustrated when faced with negotiating in a culture in many ways quite opposite from the world "back home." In this book I have tried to simplify negotiating by describing it both as it may apply in America and then by comparing it to how it may work in Korea.

Whenever one generalizes across cultures there is a distinct danger of failing to account for notable exceptions. I ask the reader to keep in mind that while the concepts contained within this book are powerful rules of thumb, negotiating will always contain an element of individuality that must be factored into the equation. Use this book as a benchmark to guide you through the complex but fascinating world of cross-cultural negotiation.

I must always thank my family for providing encouragement and support through the more than two years I worked on this book. They have contributed in ways difficult to describe in these short paragraphs.

This is my fifth book published in a long relationship with Hollym Publishers. Writing a book is a long arduous process and is never accomplished alone. Every author relies on a number of people to help transform his ideas into a professional publication. My editor Julie Han, along with the wonderful staff at Hollym, have been a great instrument in making this book possible.

I have worked with Julie Han for several years and owe her a huge debt in facilitating much of my work. Finally, I wish to thank Almighty God for whatever good will come from this publication. Through God's grace I have been blessed with the spirit to complete another project. I sincerely hope it will help people of both countries understand each other and work together in a true spirit of cooperation.

About the Author

R ichard Saccone has lived and worked in Korea for over 13 years since first arriving in 1978. Over the years he appeared regularly on television, radio and for awhile, wrote a weekly travel column. In 1995, he assisted the BBC in preparing a special television travel program on Gyeongju. In addition, Mr. Saccone has worked in several different business positions in Korea. His sincere interest in the culture and history of this country motivated him to write five books on Korea. He has travelled throughout the peninsula like no other foreigner.

Always eager to share his knowledge and experience, Mr. Saccone, through his writing, continues to create interest about Korea among foreigners. Originally from Pittsburgh, Pennsylvania, he earned academic degrees from Weber State University (B.S.), Naval Postgraduate School (M.A.), and the University of Oklahoma (M.P.A.).

CONTENTS

CHAPTER 4.

Understanding Each Others Culture

CHAPTER 5.

Common Negotiating Tactics/ Techniques (and counters)

CHAPTER 6.
Successfully Negotiating with Koreans ⋯⋯ 119

CHAPTER 7.
Situational Negotiations (Examples) ⋯⋯ 157

CHAPTER 8.
Negotiating with Bureaucrats ⋯⋯⋯ 163

CHAPTER 10.
Putting It All Together ⋯⋯⋯ 169

Introduction to Negotiation

CHAPTER 1

Introduction to Negotiation

"To confer with another so as to arrive at the settlement of some matter." There are quite a few variations to the definition of negotiation, but this simple one serves us best. Individuals have a variety of perceptions about the word negotiation. Most imagine a dimly lit room with serious faced figures seated across a clean table formally presenting arguments. Take a closer look at the definition. Think about it for a moment and you will conclude that what we define as negotiation is much more encompassing and is performed nearly every day by almost every one of us. We negotiate in almost all aspects of our lives. If you are still stuck in the traditional paradigm you can probably think of examples such as negotiating to buy a new car, negotiating salary and raises at work, or negotiating the price of an item at a flea market.

Keep thinking and you will likely discover that you also negotiate with your family over who will use the car today, what TV shows you'll watch, where you will spend the family vacation this year and much more. You negotiate with your friends about what to do and where to go. At work you negotiate times and dates of appointments, meetings, deliveries and a score of other matters. You probably even negotiate with the traffic officer when pulled over for a violation. If you really thought about it, you would discover that negotiations are already an integral part of your day. In addition, a number of us negotiate more formally in business or government as described above. Now, ask yourself, would life be better if I could negotiate more effectively? The answer should be an undeniable yes.

This is only one facet of the subject however. Even with the permeation of negotiation in our lives I suggest negotiation will become an even more powerful influence when you add this maxim "**Everything is negotiable**." I mean it. Most Americans, who haven't yet realized the importance of this little phrase, will be incredulous at my assertion. Of course, I am not the first to say it but I will try to be the one that convinces you of it. Americans more than others, grow up in a marketplace of fixed prices that we have come to view with a "take it or leave it" mentality. Many of us routinely concede our bargaining position allowing ourselves to be falsely convinced we have no choice. The truth is, once you realize that everything is negotiable and learn how to negotiate effectively, a whole new perspective on life will emerge. Opportunities will sprout seemingly from nowhere and your ability to earn more and spend less will literally astound and please you. No longer will you automatically agree to pay the asking price for anything and no longer will you be an inept seller. But negotiating is not just about buying and selling, it is about getting what you want. It could be about changing policies, convincing someone to do you a favor, or arranging that special date, the applications are limitless. Learning to negotiate will change your life.

But the title of this book deals with negotiating in Korea. I mentioned before that even though Americans grow up in an atmosphere of perceived fixed prices, negotiation possibilities are almost unlimited. Korea is a society based on negotiation and the opportunities are even more apparent than in America. So whether you're shopping in It'aewon, or working out a joint venture business deal, buying your groceries, purchasing a car, discussing the rent or key money,[1] considering the interest rate on a potential loan, thinking of how to increase your salary, making hotel reservations or taking a taxi to lunch, you should be negotiating. When your car breaks down, negotiate the repairs. When you have an accident, do as most Koreans and negotiate the damages. Workers negotiate with their subordinates and superiors. Managers negotiate with employees, buyers, contractors, and government officials. In large companies various departments negotiate with each other, the list is endless. If you are living, traveling or working in Korea or with Koreans, your negotiation skills are even more important and will make an even larger difference in your ability to reach your goal. As you will quickly see, Korea is the land of bargaining. People are predisposed to bargain and a smart buyer can reap huge benefits. Like Americans, Koreans in general tend to have a formal perception of the word negotiation and fail to realize just how often they actually use negotiation skills. Like Americans, most Koreans utilize only the rudimentary techniques, and only a few of the large number of techniques at their disposal.

But will the techniques most often used by Americans work in Korea? It turns out that some will and some won't. Other techniques are cross culturally effective but should be delivered differently and a few must be completely revised. This book will attempt to discuss a variety of techniques that will give you spot opportunities to negotiate and provide the skills to take full

---

[1] Key money is a Korean system of renting where the renter places a large deposit (ex $100,000) with a landlord while the renter lives in the apartment for a fixed term (1-2 years). At the end of the term, the landlord returns the deposit to the renter. In effect the renter has lived rent free, and the landlord has made money from the interest of the deposit.

advantage of them. Culture plays an enormous role in negotiation and I will discuss cultural differences that will help you negotiate more effectively in Korea. So whether you consider yourself an amateur or an accomplished negotiator there is information within these pages that will help you be more effective.

MYTHS OF NEGOTIATION

People cling to a number of myths and stereotypes about negotiation which prevents them from using negotiation skills to their full advantage.

Myth 1 You only negotiate in certain situations. For example, it's acceptable to negotiate at a flea market but not in a restaurant, or it's OK to negotiate for group rates but not individual discounts.

These paradigms unnecessarily limit the use of negotiation. Just because negotiation does not mean you will always do as well as you like, but by negotiating whenever possible, you will increase your advantages and overall winnings.

Myth 2 Negotiating is only performed at conference tables.

Nothing could be further from the truth. Negotiation is conducted everywhere including conference tables.

Myth 3 Negotiation requires formal training.

Wrong again! Of course formal training can be helpful but some of the most successful negotiators are self-taught in the school of life.

Myth 4 Negotiation is new.

In fact, we might add it to the list claiming to be the second oldest profession. The first recorded negotiation can be found in the Bible. Genesis 18:24-33, details Abraham negotiating with God Himself to save Sodom and Gomorrah. By the way, Abraham successfully persuaded God to agree to save the city if only ten good people could be found. The original offer was 50.

Myth 5 Negotiation is formal.

Some negotiations between countries or certain legal negotiations can be very formal. But remember that negotiation doesn't need to be formal and, in fact, there is much to be gained by keeping negotiations relatively informal.

Fundamentals of Negotiation

CHAPTER 2
Fundamentals of Negotiation

It should come as no surprise to Americans that the key to master negotiations truly begins at performing the basics well. Legendary professional football coach George Allen, who coached the Washington Redskins to a Super Bowl said, "Everyone who does well does so because they mastered the fundamentals." Most leaders and successful people insist as much. The principle similarly applies to negotiations. Some of the fundamentals are discussed in this chapter so take the time to master them.

Think of negotiation as merely a conversation. It involves two or more people exchanging their views about a matter of mutual interest. By using this casual, more informal view of the process it can be made simpler and considerably less intimidating.

A. TIMING - KNOW WHEN TO NEGOTIATE

Recognizing, or actually creating, the opportunity to negotiate can mean the difference among success, partial success and failure. How many times have you walked into a store and paid the listed price without question? Train yourself to quietly ask, how can I negotiate in this situation? Then actually try it.

Another aspect of timing is beginning a negotiation when

it's right for you and the NP. Choose a time when the NP can devote his full attention to the matter. I remember shopping in Itaewon for a pair of golf shoes with a friend. He selected a pair which suited his taste and began to bargain with the sales person. After a few minutes they had narrowed the price difference to about $5.00. About that time a bus full of Japanese tourists arrived. The customers streamed in and started buying sets of golf clubs. The sales person completely forgot about my friend and attended the higher spending customers. My friend became angry and argued that he was there first, but he was politely disregarded. Talking about it later, he realized the importance of timing. The sales person could not afford to bargain over such a small sale when faced with the prospect of selling dozens of sets of the higher priced clubs. In a retail setting, catching your NP at the right moment will make a difference. Think of similar examples in other negotiating settings. Would you ask your boss for a raise after you heard him arguing with corporate headquarters on the telephone? Would you ask a favor of a friend who just had an auto accident or a bad day at work? It sounds like common sense but I have seen scores of instances where timing was foolishly disregarded because one side was either impatient or so emotional about their desires that they could not contain themselves. In more formal negotiations, you may have to create or ensure proper timing by putting the NP in the proper mood. When negotiating with Koreans this point shines in significance. Koreans place great emphasis on mood and personal feelings. If an appropriate time is too difficult to arrange at the moment, and you determine a scheduled negotiating session would not be to your advantage, consider postponing or delaying it until a more opportune time. Always prepare for delays. Negotiations can last a few minutes or a few years so have an idea of the possible length before beginning and include extra time, in the plan, for unexpected delays.

Another aspect of proper timing involves knowing when to stop. If you discover a negotiation was initiated at the wrong time or circumstances changed making an ongoing negotiation unproductive, don't be afraid to suggest temporarily halting the negotiation and postponing it to a more suitable time.

How about re-negotiating? The same rule applies. Plan to re-negotiate at key points when both sides are satisfied with the relationship, like just after a major success. Take advantage of good times to re-negotiate and don't be afraid to include provisions for re-negotiation into an initial contract. The truth is, you can control the timing of most re-negotiations. You know when a lease expires, when it is time to buy a new car, or when the labor contract is coming up for review. Prepare for the discussion and initiate negotiations when it is most beneficial to you. When negotiating in Korea, don't forget one more possible obstacle, holidays. American businessmen don't often schedule negotiations to begin around Christmas, New Years or other important American holidays. The same is true in Korea. Koreans celebrate a few special holidays that entail important family obligations. Two of the most important Korean holidays are Chuseok and Seollal. They are the equivalent to our Thanksgiving and New Years respectively. The entire country shuts down during these two periods. Both are usually celebrated as multi-day holidays in conjunction with a weekend so plan on an entire week of business inactivity. Another interesting point about these holidays is that they do not fall on exactly the same date each year. Their celebration is determined by the lunar calendar so they are changed slightly from year to year. Be careful not to schedule negotiations too close to either of these periods. Take notice of the other Korean Holidays as well. Some are celebrated according to the lunar calendar and some by the solar calendar. An abbreviated list is provided for your convenience.

Korean National Holidays

Name	National Holidays
New Year's Day **(1 January)**	The first day of the year is really a Western holiday. More and more Koreans are celebrating it as they once celebrated the Lunar New Year. However, there is one tradition that is performed exclusively on New Year's Eve. Every year, large crowds gather at Bosingak in downtown Seoul on Jongno. In the pavilion hangs the great bell that rings in the new year for Koreans. A ceremony is conducted and the bell is rung 33 times at midnight. The streets in the vicinity are closed as they are jammed with crowds of merry makers. New Year's Eve parties are not common in Korea as they are in America. Korean throw "end of year" parties in the latter part of December but not necessarily New Year's Eve.
Lunar New Year's Day **(1 January by the lunar calender)**	One of the most important holidays in Korea, Seollal (lunar New Year's day) is second only to Ch'useok (Korean Thanksgiving) in importance to Koreans. During Seollal, families all over the peninsula gather to pay homage to their ancestors and perform many interesting and traditional ceremonies and rituals. One custom foreigners often see pictures of is the *sebae*, which requires family members to bow low to the floor to their elders. This is performed at home and at the graves of their ancestors. Seollal is full of wonderful color and family members often choose to wear their brightly colored *hanbok*, traditional Korean costumes. Both men and women wear *hanbok* but it seems the women's are more decorative and individualized. If you are out and about on this day you will have a chance for some

wonderful photos of Koreans wearing *hanbok* but always remember to ask permission so as not to offend.

Of course in the homes there is plenty to eat including *buchim* (a kind of pancake), *tteokkuk* (rice cake soup), and traditional rice cakes. After eating *tteokkuk* Koreans say you are officially one year older. Following all the feasting, family members and guests often play games such as *yut nori*, an interesting game with four uneven pegs that are tossed for points. *Yut nori* is popular and easy to learn so try if you get the chance.

This special day is part of a three day holiday which allows families to spend more time together and perform the required rituals to their ancestors. So many city dwellers must return to their hometowns in the countryside.

Independence Day (1 March)

While we celebrate the birth of our nation the Korean Independence Day celebrates the birth of a movement to fight against the oppression of the Japanese. From 1910-1945 the Japanese colonized Korea and subjected the people to unbelievable oppression. On the first of March, 1919 some patriotic leaders read a declaration of independence in Pagoda Park, in downtown Seoul, that initiated and independence movement throughout the nation. The movement lasted until eventual liberation in 1945. Every year the hisoric declaration is read at Tapgol Park, in downtown Seoul, in memory of the event.

Arbor Day (5 April)

A sense of community is fostered. And natural resources are replenished by encouraging everyone to plant a tree.

Buddha's Birthday (8 April by the lunar calender)

A colorful religious holiday, Buddhist temples around the country, hang lanterns around the temple grounds and march through town in colorful parades. The largest celebration may be in Seoul shere a huge parade, from Yeoeuido Island to Jogye Temple in the downtown, highlights the festivities. While it is a religious celebration, visitors are welcome but encouraged to respect the solemn ceremonies. Seminars and cultural shows are also conducted at separate locations. This holiday may fall anywhere in April or May by the solar calendar.

Children's Day **(5 Day)**	Established to promote the health and happiness of children, this special day has grown into a popular holiday. It's a time for parents to spend with their kids. For the kids, it's a day to receive special attention. The country's amusement parks and playgrounds are packed with children so prepare for the crowds before you venture out.
Memorial Day **(6 June)**	A solemn occasion steeped in ceremony to honor those who died serving their country. The nation's cemeteries and war monuments often conduct special programs on this day.
Constitution Day **(17 July)**	Three years after the liberation from Japan, a new government was formed in 1948. This holiday essentially celebrates the formation of the Republic of Korea.
Liberation Day **(15 August)**	The tremendous joy at the liberation from Japan, after thirty-five years of colonial rule, is remembered on this special holiday.
Chuseok **(15 August by the** **lunar calender)**	It is often compared to American Thanksgiving as it is a harvest celebration, bringing families together to share traditional foods and observe traditional customs. Chuseok is different in that family members must also honor an obligation to return to their hometown to worship their ancestors. This movement of people causes severe traffic snarls as literally tens of millions make the pilgrimage back to their hometowns. For good luck, everyone is expected to eat *songpyeon*, little dumpling style rice cakes shaped like half moons, in addition to many other traditional dishes. It is certainly one of the oldest and probably the most important of the nation's holidays. Usually lasting three days, Chuseok falls sometime in August or September by the solar calendar.

National Foundation Day (3 October)	Koreans commenmorate the founding of ancient Korea, which according to legend, occurred around 2333 B.C. by the mythical character known as Dangun. In Seoul special ceremonies are held in Sajik Park in the downtown area.
Christmas (25 December)	A Western style Christmas is growing more popular in Korea. Decorations, gift exchange, department store sales and religious ceremonies are all part of the holiday season. While the following additional entries are not national holidays they are similar in many ways to American holidays.

Name	Holidays
Valentines Day (14 February)	In Korea this is a day when ladies give their sweethearts chocolates or other tokens of affection.
White Day (14 March)	Men get their chance to show their affection by offering candy or small gifts to the ones they love.
Parents' Day (8 May)	Unlike America which has a separate Mother's and Father's Day, Koreans combine them and honor both on Parents' Day.
Armed Forces Day (1 October)	The Armed Forces are remembered by an extravagant parade with military marching bands, soldiers, tanks, planes, and a variety of equipment looking it's best and passing in review through the downtown section of Seoul. The parade has been limited to once every three years and if you are in Korea during that time make sure and see it.
Korean Alphabet Day (9 October)	The Korean alphabet (Hangeul) was developed under the direction of Korea's most famous King (King Sejong) in 1446. Koreans are proud of their alphabet and celebrate the holiday with concerts and cultural events.

B. Understanding People - Personalities affect negotiations

People negotiate, not governments or corporations. Personalities and culture affect negotiations so knowledge of human behavior is essential to cross cultural negotiation. Facts, perception, style, ego, circumstance and other factors combine in a slightly different mixture in every instance. For both Koreans and Americans, negotiation is often linked to self-esteem. If we do poorly, we often perceive it as a reflection of our personal worth. Of course this is not necessarily rational but it is often reality. When you add the complexities of inter-cultural negotiation, self esteem becomes an even more critical factor. Negotiation is often mistakenly viewed as merely a series of proposals and counter proposals, but of course it is far more. Negotiation is a process of information and goal satisfaction that should always be as dynamic as possible. Goals include personal, corporate and professional, so understanding the NP and his goals is essential.

Books on negotiation often include information on motivational theory and the basics of personality theory, as they should. The key to negotiation is often hidden within the personality of the negotiator. Assumptions are an important part of the NP's personality. Be aware of NP's assumptions because they frame that person's way of thinking. Assumptions are not always easy to discern. We are often unaware of our own assumptions and are unable to trace their origins or effects. In his book on negotiation, Nierenberg uses an appropriate example of hidden assumptions. "I saw a beggar coming out of the ladies room." Upon reading this you might have been alarmed

---

[2] Gerard I. Nierenberg, *The Art of Negotiating* (New York: Barnes & Noble Inc., 1968), p 63.

if your hidden assumption was that beggars are men.[2] Everyone has hidden assumptions, if you can surface and identify them it can help immensely in the negotiation. *Maslow's hierarchy* of needs is cross-cultural. People of most cultures must satisfy the safety and security needs before satisfying those of belonging and self-actualization. Also, remember when negotiating there are two types of needs, the needs of the organization and the negotiator. Both need to be recognized and attended to. In Korea, a large number of business executives came to business after a distinguished career in the Korean military. While their numbers are constantly reducing, they still form a huge cadre among the ranks of businessmen. Keep that background in mind while negotiating with them. Don't neglect to consider your NP's political beliefs. They are important to understanding his psyche. Never preach your beliefs to the NP but try to understand and at least acknowledge his.

Abraham Maslow wrote the defining theory of motivation when he designed his hierarchy of needs (shown in diagram). The five levels of human needs he described formed a pyramid to illustrate both the frequency and level of human motivational development. The most common and most basic needs (physiological) include hunger, thirst, and sex. Safety needs include security, freedom from fear, desire for structure, law and order among others. Moving up one more level we encounter the (social) needs which include belongingness and love. Loneliness and rejection of the group will be avoided at this level. Esteem needs encompass the human desire for respect and acknowledgement. Finally, Maslow believed all humans desire for respect and acknowledgement. Finally, Maslow believed all humans desire to self-actualize, meaning to achieve at a level where that person is at peace with himself.[3]

All these needs are important in negotiation. It can be argued that in Korea, the Social and Esteem needs may be switched to more accurately portray Korean emphasis on the group in society. Regardless, every negotiator must consider the human needs of the NP to be effective.

Maslow's Hierarchy of Needs

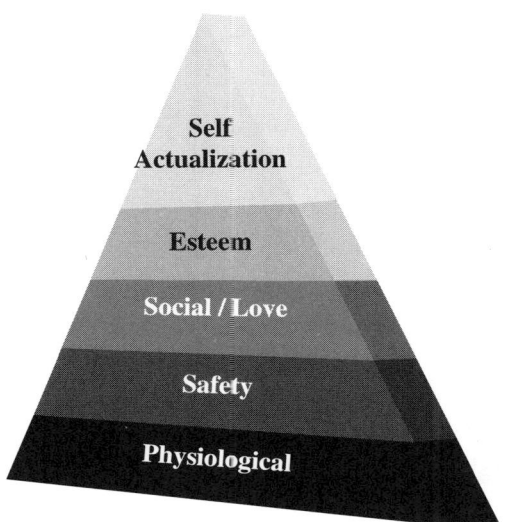

C. LISTENING - BE A GOOD LISTENER

How many books emphasize this? The truth is people pay lip service to listening yet all, including the experts, acknowledge it's importance. The most common and most annoying characteristic of poor listeners is interrupting. Never interrupt — first

---

[3] Maslow, Abraham, *Motivation & Personality*, 2nd edition (Harper & Row, 1970).

of all it's rude in any culture, but it is doubly rude in Korea if the NP is older than you are or in a more senior social position. Secondly, your NP doesn't want to hear you, he wants to hear himself. You lose respect by interrupting. I knew an executive who was considered a fairly capable salesman. He had immense natural ability and was considered a successful businessman. Unfortunately, he had the annoying habit of interrupting his clients. I don't think he even realized it. He alienated quite a few clients with his interrupting. He often managed to overcome this fault with his other talents but I sometimes wondered how many clients he might have saved had he just been able to listen better. Always let the other person have their say.

Obviously, effective listening goes beyond not interrupting. An effective listener makes the NP feel he is truly trying to understand him. This is achieved with verbal and non-verbal attention. Verbal attention requires well-timed yes's or empathetic sighs. Non-verbal attention requires proper body posture to convey sincerity. Most people are busy with formulating their response before the other person has finished speaking. Don't be so absorbed in making your point that you miss the hints and subtle signals the other side is sending. Listen with your "eyes" and ears. Listen for needs, what he says/the way he says it/ask questions. Ask yourself. Are you hearing only what you want to hear? This is especially important in Korea where the message is often communicated indirectly. Listening more and speaking less can truly lead to a better negotiation and a more agreeable partner.

Judge a man by his questions rather than his answers.
— Voltaire

D. ASKING QUESTIONS -FORMULATE HIGH QUALITY QUESTIONS

Second only to listening in importance, formulating high quality questions is, in a sense, part of listening. Well-timed and well-stated questions can convince the NP you are trying to understand his side. High quality questions also help sharpen your arguments. Of course there are several types of questions. Knowing which question to use, as well as the proper timing, affects the outcome.

Probing questions are designed to stimulate discussion. Conversation can broaden the possibility that the NP will reveal information about himself, or his negotiating position, which you may use to your advantage. These questions should be open-ended and usually start with a question word like how, why, and what etc. To ensure understanding, repeat the question later in the conversation or ask the same question in a different way, and compare responses.

Ask the NP for feelings. Ask how he reacted, or what he was thinking. Pose general questions in the beginning and progress to the more specific. Do not return to general questions after the issue has been closed or you may allow the NP to reopen discussion in undesirable areas.

Don't be afraid to ask for clarification. Koreans generally are embarrassed to ask someone to repeat a question. I have seen negotiators neglect to ask questions that could have developed information helpful to their position, because they were too embarrassed. Any topic may be subject to questioning; if given a deadline ask why, if quoted a price ask how they arrived at that figure. More importantly, ask for restatement when the NP submits claims you don't agree with. Question their "facts." Sometimes we concede facts that aren't correct. Tell the NP you don't understand or mention that your data indicates something different. Ask how the NP calculated his figures. For example, if the NP offers to complete a task in two months ask him to explain how he arrived at that figure. Then you may present your rationale for why it could be completed in less time. Always remember never to pose a question as an accusation. Some negotiators sound accusatory without realizing it. Approach the situation as an interesting puzzle that must be solved by both sides, don't be confrontational or force the NP on the defensive. Strive to question without causing the NP to feel distrusted.

It's important to ask questions that are not embarrassing. Do not cause the Korean NP to lose face. When communicating across cultures it is imperative to ask questions that help clarify key points. Difficult concepts should be verified two or three times to insure both sides are truly in agreement.

Some questions are answered better by persons than the NP. Business associates and competitors may often provide valuable information about the NP. As a fraud investigator I learned it was common for a company's competitors to provide valuable information about another company's operations, problems, or dirty tricks. They were also eager to provide delicate information about key personnel. Of course such information must also be independently verified but competitors frequently provide a solid starting point from which to gather even more information.

Be careful not to ask loaded questions, you know, the questions that contain a major assumption that may or may not be true. Tele-marketers and car salesmen love to ask them. Before you have agreed to buy anything, the car salesman asks as he begins filling out the paperwork, "Now who will be driving this car, you or the wife?" Don't be intimidated by such questions. Refuse to accept the basic premise and force the question to be restated or restate it yourself.

Implied demand / counter demand questions are also commonly used. The implied demand question is used to apply pressure to an opponent. For example, "If I buy this stereo, will you include some cassette tapes for free?" When the NP presents a question, which includes a demand, counter with a demanding question of your own. (Demand from buyer) "If I buy this stereo will you throw in some cassette tapes?" (Counter demand from seller) "If I include the tapes will you buy right now?"

Some negotiators pose questions that serve to educate an NP. For example, "Did you know our company has twenty-five Fortune 500 clients? Did you see our company Chairman on television yesterday with the President of your country?" Such questions are an indirect way to inform the NP about key facts that may impress the NP and boost your perceived status. This could provide needed leverage during a negotiation.

Most negotiators agree that questions should perform the following functions:

Chart of what questions should perform

Function	Examples of questions
Get attention	What if I could offer this product at half the list price?
Get information	What are your ideas for solving this problem?
Give information	Do you realize how angry the boss is because you missed the deadline?
Start a person thinking	How could we satisfy your interests as well as mine?
Get them to reach their own conclusions	Isn't the solution similar to what you originally suggested?
Bring to a conclusion	Considering all the points of agreement, shouldn't we finalize this contract right now?

Phrasing can be as important as content and timing. Choose your words carefully; try to pose questions that elicit a positive response. Remember the example of the clergyman's question - which one could you answer yes to. May I smoke while praying? May I pray while smoking? The answer to the former is no, the latter is yes.

Remember to keep negative emotions out of questions. Positive emotions are useful however. A smiling face and youthful exuberance can make a question more appealing.

E. DEALING WITH OBSTACLES (DEADLOCKS & IMPASSES)

Begin negotiating the easy issues and try to find as many areas of agreement as possible. This will allow you to obtain a larger percentage of yes answers to your proposals. Initial agreement between both sides sets a positive mood for the negotiation. If the Korean NP is used to agreeing with you in the early stages it will be easier to reach agreement when the more difficult issues surface in the later stages.

Offer Alternatives - Conflicts often develop when neither side can see a way to conclude favorably. If the solutions were obvious more conflicts would have happy endings. Since solutions are often complex, negotiators must search for creative alternatives to reach resolution. The often-told story of the 18th camel illustrates this point so very well. The story goes like this; A rich man died and left behind three sons. As their inheritance he left 17 camels to be divided as follows; 1/2 to the first son, 1/3 to the second son and 1/9 to the last son. Since the camels could not be divided evenly the sons began to quarrel over the inheritance. The struggle became so heated that it threatened the relationship between the brothers. The men decided to take their problem to a wise old woman who listened patiently and offered this solution. She said "take my camel and add it to your own and then divide the inheritance." The brothers took the extra camel and now, with 18 camels, they divided the inheritance. The first son took 1/2 or nine camels, the second took 1/3 or six camels, the last son took 1/9 or two camels. Nine, six and two equals 17 camels so the men returned the 18th camel back to the wise old woman. Their problem was solved by a <u>creative solution</u>.

Creative solutions are discovered by examining the problem from different angles. Ask others to look at the situation and offer suggestions. A "fresh set of eyes" can often spark creativity. Changing the location or environment may also spur new ideas. In Korea, it is not uncommon to relocate a meeting to the golf course or a drinking establishment. Use any environment that will allow the NP to feel more comfortable and less threatened. One more suggestion is to introduce a third party, totally disconnected from your negotiation or even your business. It is surprising how outsiders can offer some of the simplest answers to a nagging problem.

If possible, try to develop multiple solutions to a negotiation. Offer several alternatives to the Korean NP and let the NP choose. This will allow the NP the feeling that he won.

Deadlocks - When two sides just cannot seem to move forward, it is wise to return to the basics. Be careful to review the basics unemotionally. Koreans do not respond positively to pressure. Be sure the other side understands the value of what you offer, if not; go over the facts again. Consider additional changes that could spark movement. Changing key negotiators or moving the location can often change the entire mood of the process. If you are stuck in a rut, don't continue to repeat your actions over and over hoping they will magically produce a breakthrough. Take a close look at your techniques and consider new approaches. This may or may not include concessions but it's usually better to save concessions as a last resort. Offering unilateral concessions at a deadlock can be risky if the deadlock occurs early in the process. However, making a concession may be a "deal closer" if proposed at the proper time.

The key to breaking deadlocks often lies in clearly defining the problems or differences and working together to solve them. Determine the NP's goals and include them in the solution. For example, if the NP says his budget is zero, your answer should be "I can work with that." Then proceed to explore alternatives that might be to his advantage. I remember encountering a Korean Company president who insisted he had no budget for a certain project. By keeping the negotiation positive and after explaining to him how necessary the project was for his company, he agreed to transfer money from another part of the budget to fund the project. Even the toughest Korean NP's enjoy working with positive, friendly foreigners.

Propose a face saving offer. There are times when the discussions begin to stiffen and tension clearly develops. It is possible to change the mood by telling a humorous story or comment. However, shy away from jokes with a punch line as most traditional jokes do not translate well and are too difficult to follow cross culturally. A well-timed humorous phrase or short story can be highly effective and easy to understand.

Impasse - When facing an impasse, re-strengthen your relationship with the NP. This is quite important to your Korean counterpart. Focus on the positive; review your accomplishments together. If you had taken the time to develop a strong relationship in advance, you are in luck, if not you are in trouble. Try switching the scenery. Suggest meeting for dinner and a night of drinking to help lighten the mood. In Korea, a surprising number of agreements are sealed at Room Salons, and other drinking establishments, rather than conference rooms. At an impasse, consider putting troublesome issues aside for later discussion. Continue to negotiate the issues you can agree on, building the sense of partnership. Consider using team members or a third party to discover if there is some other hidden issue causing difficulty. An impasse could result if the NP somehow lost face during the negotiation. This may not be readily apparent. It can sometimes be discovered and resolved by a third party without surfacing it publicly.

F. Personal Attacks

> *I hold it to be a proof of great prudence for men to abstain*
> *from threats and insults.*
> — Machiavelli

Deflect or ignore personal attacks. Opponents may try to push your "hot buttons" to see your reaction or destroy your focus. Such tactics may be disguised in humor. Opponents may play to an audience if the opportunity arises. The counter is to call them on it. Turn the tables on the NP if possible. Attacks on you or your proposals may be turned into opportunities to put you both on the same side. I remember overhearing a supervisor chastising a younger employee about a suggestion. "Don't you know this will never work, Don't you know we tried this two years ago and failed, of course not, you're too young," he cruelly said to the young man. The reply was a textbook case in tact. "You are right" he said, "I didn't know about that. You have been here a long time. Would you fill me in on some of the history and your opinions about what went wrong with this proposal in the past so I can be sure to tackle those problems this time around." The smooth unemotional answer took the wind right out of the supervisor's sails.

Don't accept a negative attack. The NP may focus on one or two mistakes you made in the past. Use every opportunity to present yourself as a "good guy." Negotiate in good faith and refrain from painting the Korean NP as the "bad guy." In a negotiation there can be more than one good guy but ensure you are one of them. Your Korean NP will respect you as a gentleman and an honest person. Finally, never initiate a personal attack. No matter how angry you become, maintain your composure. If you maintain emotional control and professionalism, your Korean NP will respect you.

COUNTER TECHNIQUE

You can appeal to one of Maslow's needs such as esteem, belonging, safety, and self-actualization. As previously stated, determine where the NP is most receptive. Avoid emotion; refocus the discussion on issues, not personalities.

G. TURNING NEGATIVES INTO POSITIVES

Negatives are common obstacles in both Eastern and Western cultures. Experienced negotiators encounter similar phrases that can stop a good idea dead in it's tracks. Rather than confronting the negative statements, understand that they represent feelings and fears that must be addressed. Attempt to turn negative statements around by rewording them in a more positive way. Continue negotiating while emphasizing positive themes and don't be discouraged. The following chart includes some of the most common phrases that are potential deal breakers. You may be able to add a few expressions of your

Chart of Negatives to Positives

Negatives	Positives
It will never work.	Let's give it a try.
It's always been done this way.	How about a new approach?
This is SOP.	This requires separate consideration.
It is good enough.	There is <u>always</u> room for improvement.
We have never done it before.	We have the chance to do it <u>first</u>.
You can't do that.	We are confident we can do it.
We tried that once.	Let's try it again <u>differently</u>.
It's not for us.	We should look at it again.
We don't have the resources.	Can we improvise?
There is no way.	Can we think of some <u>alternatives</u>?
It can't be done.	Anything is possible.
It's too difficult.	I'm excited by the challenge.
They won't listen.	Open some new channels of communication.
I don't like a lot of changes.	I like to learn something new.
Sounds too risky.	The chance is <u>worth</u> it.
It won't fly.	We must <u>try</u> to know for sure.
They won't like it.	Show them the opportunities.
It's beyond our ability.	<u>Nothing</u> can stop this team.
If it ain't broke don't fix it.	We can <u>improve</u> it.
Someone else is already doing it.	We will do it better.
It's impossible.	Together <u>we</u> can make it happen.
It won't work.	Let me show you how it <u>will</u> work.

own.

At the same time present your ideas in a positive framework. Negative statements can place you in a perilous negotiating position. If selling you might say, "I won't accept anything less than $30,000 for this equipment." Such a position however, could prove too discouraging to the NP. Instead, you will make a better impression with something like, "I am willing to sell this equipment for $30,000. It is simple and unemotional. It also communicates less finality and invites negotiation."

Don't be afraid to let some unresolved issues remain. In the end, if you have reached 95% agreement, then agree on that and leave the other 5% for separate discussion.

H. TESTING FOR HONESTY

Before, during and after a negotiation you must test NP for honesty. Testing is a continuous process. Use known information to ask questions that will indicate if NP is truthful and trustworthy. If you discover dishonesty, it is often better not to disclose it. In rare cases, when you intend to totally break relations it may be to your advantage to confront the dishonesty. In no case is it wise to disclose the fact that you were testing the NP. At the very least, such information will ruin the relationship, but it could also damage future negotiations with other Koreans and may even provoke countermeasures against you or your company.

It is not uncommon for Korean companies to approach another company under the guise of doing business with the real intent of merely gathering information. The NP will use the promise of a lucrative deal to convince you to disclose more information about your company than you would normally reveal. This tactic is certainly unethical but remember it is not limited to small companies. Large conglomerates have been guilty of the same techniques as well as even more serious and highly publicized cases of industrial espionage.

I. NEVER TAKE THE FIRST OFFER

No matter how good it looks the first offer is just a starting point. Americans are too often in a rush to conclude business so if the first offer sounds reasonable they quickly agree and try to wrap up the proceedings. This is a huge mistake. Always negotiate further. The worst that could happen is you may end up accepting the original offer but you just might get all that you ask for. A few years ago I was traveling on vacation with my family. On my return trip to Korea we had to change planes at Narita Airport in Japan. We had just settled into our seats when an airline official boarded the aircraft and announced the flight to Seoul was over booked and requested eight volunteers disembark and take the next flight at the same time the following day. He offered to pay $200 per seat and provide hotel accommodations for the night including a free dinner. A couple of hands quickly went up, then a couple more and soon four people were quickly taken from the plane. The man was left in need of four more seats. I asked if I could speak to him. I explained that with my wife and two children we could take all four seats and solve his problem but it would be a bit inconvenient for us. I said I was wondering if he would include breakfast the next morning and upgrade us to first class the next day. He gladly consented to my request. He deeply appreciated it. A few months later while traveling on business he spotted me at the airport and took the time to come over and talk with me. Without asking, he again upgraded me to first class all the way back to the United States. Now remember, four people got off the airplane just before me, without the added benefits I negotiated, all because they took the first offer and neglected to ask for a better deal. When an opportunity to negotiate arises, <u>slow down, determine what you want and start the conversation</u>.

If a person accepts the first offer he usually becomes unhappy later. The person will likely think either something is wrong with the product or he could have bargained for a better deal— it's human nature. If for no other reason than your own peace of mind, don't accept the first offer.

During a move from one apartment to another in Seoul I wanted to dispose of some of my furniture. After shopping around a little I discovered my old dresser was worth about $420 and several other pieces were of similar value. I contacted a used furniture salesman who visited my house, looked at my dresser and offered me - you guessed it - $420. Tempted to take the offer and be done with it, instead I looked at him with a serious face and said simply, "You will have to do better than that." He thought for a while and eventually made a deal for the whole set, which was quite more than I had expected.

J. MAKING AN OFFER

Considerable debate has transpired, in negotiation literature, as to who should offer first. Most experts advise against making the first offer. However, there are times when it's advantageous. The first offer can frame a negotiation, and establish benchmarks and parameters that can be to your benefit. There are also dangers. If the first offer is too high the NP may decide there is no use continuing and quit. This illustrates well the purpose of preparation and intelligence about the NP. It is important to try and discover what the approximate range of his bargaining position, if possible. Knowing this in advance could prevent a NP from walking away because of a "show stopping" offer unknowingly presented. Eventually, in any negotiation you will come to the point where you will reveal your position. If the NP proposes the first offer you may decide not to accept it and silently wait for another offer (a legitimate tactic at times) or you can join the process and propose a counter offer of your own. The size and timing of your offer are critical, and should be well thought out.

There is no magic formula for making an offer, it depends on the total negotiating situation. You must assess all the factors and decide what is best in each particular situation.

> *The Prudent archer, when the place they wish to hit is too far off, knowing how far their bow will carry, aim at a spot much higher than the one they wish to hit, not in order to reach this height with the arrow, but by help of this high aim to hit the spot they wish.*
>
> — Machiavelli

If you are the seller, (or the party requesting), your first offer will naturally be high. If you want a salary increase of $3,000 you may ask for $5,000. But remember that number immediately becomes the ceiling and sets the outer limits of the negotiation. The only way to recover later is to link it to another request. For example if you wanted to revisit the initial salary request you might say "I originally requested the $5,000 based on a total package that included two weeks paid vacation. If you will only grant a one-week vacation then I must demand a

$6,000 increase." If you already know the NP's offer, an unspoken rule is to position your offer about the same distance away as theirs. For example, if you want a $2,000 raise and they are prepared to offer $1,000, you should request $3,000. With few exceptions, I don't normally recommend so-called highball or lowball offers except as a last resort. Making an extreme offer will ruin your credibility with Koreans. Your offer can be high but should be believable. In any case, always begin friendly. It is normal to go from friendly to confrontational but almost impossible to successfully change from confrontational back to friendly. Once the Korean NP becomes suspicious of your intentions it will be difficult to rebuild trust.

Don't use round numbers as they are too easy to counter. If your side offers $2,000, the NP may offer $1,000 and subsequent splits will leave you at a disadvantage. However, if your original offer was $2,022 it is more resistant to large splits. The more precise offer provides the advantage to you.

Consider "what if" offers - the offer that's not an offer. What if offers are purely hypothetical and are used to probe the NP. For example, what if I bought three sweaters, would you increase the discount to 20%? There is no guarantee you will buy three sweaters and you are not offering to buy them, you are simply asking a question. On the other hand a <u>conditional</u> offer implies a <u>commitment</u> - for example, if you promise delivery by next month we will order a three month supply.

Before phrasing an offer, carefully consider the NP's situation and personality. To keep from pressuring an NP you could phrase an offer in the form of a question - would you take $10 for this item? If you want to create pressure or communicate finality phrase the offer as a statement, I'll give you ten dollars for it.

An offer should be more than numbers, it should clearly demonstrate how it satisfies the NP's needs. If an NP asks you to build a bridge in 24 months for $20 million, instead of just saying you could build it for $19 million, first answer that you will build it in less time at a price below what he requested. This satisfies his needs, gives your offer more prestige, and provides more latitude at arriving at an actual dollar figure.

Try not to offer ranges - give specific figures. In other words, do not use figures like 10 or 12%, 2-3 months, or 5-6 billion won, unless you mean it. The NP will choose the figure that most benefits him. At the same time, you must know your own range and try to discover the range of your NP. You can use body language to communicate your message. Present an offer and keep silent! Look at your Korean NP! Wait for his response. Don't be afraid of silence. It is common for Koreans to sit in silent contemplation. Wait patiently for their response.

Don't be afraid to propose an outrageously low offer. You might just get it. I propose changing the saying that, necessity is the mother of invention, to necessity is the mother of negotiation. I remember going to a flea market with my youngest son who is a baseball card collector. He spotted a valuable Roberto Clemente card he desperately wanted and the asking price was ten dollars. My son haggled for a while and finally asked the man his lowest acceptable price, at which the man quoted five dollars. My son talked a bit longer, discussing card prices and current demand, then he boldly offered the man one dollar and surprisingly the man reluctantly accepted. Astonished at my son's negotiating prowess I asked him what made him persevere, for such an incredibly low price, even after the seller had declared his lowest acceptable price as five dollars. "It was easy dad" he replied, "I only had one dollar." How many of us would have the courage to offer such a ridiculously low amount in the same circumstances. If my son had told the man, at the beginning of the negotiation, that he only had one dollar, there probably would not have been a negotiation. By waiting for the proper moment, after both sides had invested time and effort in the process, he was able to achieve his goal.

The counter technique to an extreme offer is simply to expose it. For example, to an American you might say, "Thank you for your offer and I will consider any serious proposals." To a Korean however, this delivery would certainly be insulting. A softer counter proposal would be more effective. The delivery should be performed with a smile. Don't cause the Korean NP to lose face, use the response to encourage a second offer. This tactic will usually cause the NP to suggest another more realistic price.

When negotiators exclude the competition and force the other side to present the first offer, they receive the better bargain. That's why in certain negotiations the NP may try to eliminate the competition and prevent the buyer from shopping around. It is as common in Korea as it is in America for a car dealer to say, "If I offer you a good deal are you ready to buy today?" They do not want the buyer to compare prices with other dealers.

Individuals may try to negotiate a lower price by excluding features. After securing the desired price they try to negotiate the features back in. This technique is universally used in Korea and America.

You must convince the NP what you are offering is of value. Include variables other than price such as quality and service. Koreans are attentive to both quality and service. In general,

Koreans are willing to pay more if they perceive the quality is superior. If negotiating over products or services, the status of a higher quality item will definitely appeal to the Korean NP.

Negotiators are often discouraged by a no or similar refusal. Learn to expect rejection as most Koreans will not accept proposals on the first try. Learn to use the refusal as a starting point for further negotiation. Persistence is important whether you are asking for a date or bargaining to close an important business deal, as Koreans are likely to politely refuse the first offer. Try to determine the most appealing factors and continue by slightly rephrasing the offer. It may not be necessary to change an offer just rephrase and submit again.

K. Concessions

Is compromise or concession a weakness in Korea? Remember, each party will ascribe different values to a concession. Americans generally value compromise, while Koreans don't necessarily. Never allow a concession to sound too easy or valueless. Don't concede too quickly, the Korean NP will wonder as to the real value. What about being the first to concede, and the timing of concessions? Offering a concession can be a great way to show sincerity, if proposed at the proper moment. If the Korean NP knows you are in a clearly stronger position it may be wise to offer a small concession to show your willingness to build a relationship, reduce tension or create harmony. Try to communicate that message when offering a concession and consider an indirect delivery to your Korean NP. For example, in a team negotiation, your members could mention to NP team members that the leader will offer a concession as a gesture of good faith for relationship building. Then you can be sure the

NP team leader will know your purpose and expectation for the concession. As a rule of thumb when negotiating with Koreans, you should not concede first when operating from a clearly inferior position as it may be perceived as weakness.

Another rule of thumb is always to receive something in return for a concession, even if the reciprocation occurs much later. In the mind of Koreans, a concession will often produce a sense of obligation that need not be stated. In some instances, before conceding, it is OK to ask, as Americans commonly do, if we do that for you what can you do for us? But in most cases it should be phrased more discreetly.

Always have some concessions in mind before entering a negotiation and resist offering them too early. It has been said that it is best to offer concessions grudgingly but gracefully. Good advice! Convince your Korean NP that the concession you propose is not easily given and that you offer it for a specific purpose. Always submit it in good spirits with the intent of fostering goodwill.

Different countries are said to employ different patterns of conceding. A study showing sample patterns of concessions using $100 as an example was conducted in a number of different countries. The study assumes four possible concessions over the course of a negotiation. The patterns are as follows:

Patterns

No.	Patterns			
1	$25	$25	$25	$25
2	$50	$50	0	0
3	0	0	0	$100
4	$100	0	0	0
5	$10	$20	$30	$40
6	$40	$30	$20	$10

The person who follows pattern #3 will usually refuse to concede until the very end and then offer a large concession in one sum. The person who concedes everything up front and then holds firm with no other concessions is represented by pattern #4. A Korean executive of a magazine I once worked for often conceded using pattern #5 when selling advertisements for his magazine. He would initially quote a price and then offer some small discount. If the client resisted he would increase the discount sometimes reaching the magazines break even point. Needless to say, neither he nor our printed list of ad prices carried much credibility with our clients. For the magazine, it was important to obtain ads at almost any cost and he was willing to sacrifice quite a bit to reach that goal.

I firmly believe it is difficult to ascribe a certain pattern to one country or another. Concession patterns are personal and vary widely according to individuals. Having said that, my own informal study of Koreans tells me that Koreans who negotiate regularly are more likely to lean toward pattern #6. Other inexperienced or infrequent negotiators will respond with any of the other patterns. It is important to know your NP and try to identify possible patterns early.

What pattern applies to you? Have you thought about it yet? If you have a pattern and are not aware of it you may be conceding an advantage to your NP. Allow me to offer a suggestion that can really aid in tough negotiations with Koreans. Save one small concession until the end. If needed, offer it at the last moment to allow your Korean NP to save face and feel he has won. It is an effective technique to set up the final concession with a well-timed pause. This lends a bit of drama and importance to the moment.

Money is not the only concession, an offer of service or personal good deed are also valuable. It may be something you would have done anyway but stated openly it may become a concession. For example you might say, Well Mr. Kim, if you agree to this deal I will personally work with your representative to ensure the deliveries are made on time. No matter that you routinely do that with all your customers, it is an added service and it will create a feeling of good will. Performed properly, the NP may even know you did it to help him save face. All the better. He will appreciate your tact and that small concession will help build a stronger bond between the two of you for the future. Concessions are better made after full discussion with NP. I have witnessed NP's presenting their requests and over eager negotiators saying, "Oh I can do that virtually making a concession without thinking of it." Consider all concessions away from the table, then decide and document them carefully.

L. CLOSING THE DEAL

The final offer needs to be made with conviction. Again, it is usually better to communicate it indirectly but ensure the message is received. If you try to pressure the NP into closing or appear over eager to close, the Korean NP will balk. The closing should appear as a natural end to the discussion. Be graceful in accepting an agreement. Foster the good feeling that both sides have won. You may accomplish this by reviewing and emphasizing what both sides will gain. Because your counterparts want to know you well, count on negotiations taking longer to complete in Korea. Even if the negotiation does not end the way you wanted, end it on a positive note. Carefully nurture and strengthen the relationships you wish to eventually maintain.

Do not burn bridges as Korea is a small country and an unfavorable reputation spreads quickly. Koreans are sticklers for formality, so count on a formal ceremony of some sort to celebrate an actual agreement. The bigger the deal the larger the ceremony. At the very least you should seal any agreement with a drink and a toast.

Arrange to prepare any official documentation associated with the negotiation. Even though it requires more work it is the safest way to protect your interests. I remember a Korean landlord who presented what looked like a standard form. I rewrote his standard form incorporating the changes important to me. He eventually agreed to my standard form. Contracts, including the exact wording of individual elements should always be negotiated.

M. WALK AWAY POWER

Develop walk away power, when you lose the ability to walk away from a negotiation you are at a disadvantage. Decide on a walk away point and stick to it. Try not to reveal it to the NP unless you are using it as a threat. In Las Vegas I became a fairly good gambler by entering a casino with only as much money as I was willing to lose. I actually began with the thought that the money was already lost. I wrote it off as entertainment money. Anything I returned home with was profit. When I was winning I would periodically put a portion of the winnings aside as profit and not touch them. In effect, I was increasing my walk away point to ensure I left ahead of my original expectations. Some nights were shorter than others but after living about two years in Las Vegas I felt comfortable I won more than I lost.

Never walk into a negotiation thinking I am going to get this no matter what. If you maintain that attitude you are likely to lose. Always develop your walk away point and never betray it. You should convince the Korean NP that you want to work together but there are limits to what is beneficial to both sides. Try not to reveal, to the NP, your exact walk away point. Affix a red zone to your walk away point to warn yourself that the end is dangerously close. This will allow time to implement corrections before reaching the actual quitting point. You may change your walk away point but it is wise to carefully consider it before doing so. You can also change the NP's walk away point, by persuading him it is still in his interest to continue.

N. WHAT MAKES A GOOD NEGOTIATOR

There are a number of personal characteristics that are helpful to negotiators. A good negotiator should have integrity and an eye for character. He should love negotiating, practice patience, attention to detail, and be a good communicator, in other words, make difficult concepts easy to understand. He should have the courage to deliver an offer, and the persistence to stick with a deal until closure. He should be an interested listener, sociable, outgoing, respectable, empathetic and curious. A good negotiator must also know himself well. Before entering a negotiation he should be able to answer the following questions:

1) What are my goals?
2) What are the NP's goals?
3) How can I obtain more information about NP and the issues?
4) Are there any topics likely to stir emotion? Can I maintain control of <u>my</u> emotion?

5) Am I prepared to be patient?

6) Am I fully prepared with all the necessary facts and figures to support <u>my</u> position?

7) Have I prepared for contingencies?

A victory in negotiation need not be defined by whether you were able to gain all that you could possibly squeeze from your opponent. It may be legitimately defined by whether both sides walked away satisfied with the final agreement.

Planning and Preparation

Planning and Preparation

To be prepared is to have no anxiety.
유비무환(有備無患)
— Korean Proverb

He will win who, prepared himself, waits to take the enemy unprepared.
— Sun Tzu

A. PLANNING AND PREPARATION

How many times, before entering a negotiation, have you heard the words, let's wing it. Far too many times, negotiators from all types of backgrounds and experience assume they will perform well by using only their wits. While the experts may call it by a different name, they all agree that preparing your actions and planning a negotiation can be one of the most important investments in securing success. A few authors refer to it as gathering intelligence, another may label it deciding strategy, but I believe, whatever you call it, that planning and preparing for negotiations are all encompassing efforts that no seasoned negotiator can afford to neglect. What will my opponent do, how will he react to my proposal, what concessions may I expect, are among the thoughts that should run through your mind. Quite a bit of anxiety over uncertainty is associated with negotiation. Much of the anxiety can be minimized with preparation. In professional football, an enormous amount of time is spent gathering information about the opposing team. Scouts study prospective opponents weeks before the scheduled match, and hundreds of hours are spent reviewing game films searching for an opponent's strengths and weaknesses. A strategy is developed and the plays used in the contest are often scripted before hand. When possible, negotiations should be approached in much the same way. The more information you gather about an opponent in advance the better equipped you are to negotiate.

Most people recognize the preparation required for a complicated business deal or a diplomatic discussion but they often overlook the fact that preparing for even seemingly insignificant or unexpected negotiations also benefit the negotiator. Gathering information not only applies to things but to people. Knowing as much as possible about an opponent can often be more helpful than knowing about the issue under negotiation. If you are a seller, personal information is often the key to developing a successful strategy. For example, if you are selling a home, imagine the importance of knowing that the buyer prefers public transportation so his wife can use the car during the day. You could emphasize that the home for sale is close to the subway and major bus stops.

If you are buying, imagine the importance of discovering that the seller is in need of fast cash and would be willing to negotiate a lower price in exchange for a quick lump sum offer. Gathering detailed background information on the NP can save considerable time and big money, if accomplished properly.

Collecting personal information can be conducted in a number of ways, by directly asking the person, asking others who know him, by researching open source references, or by direct observation.

If your opponents are well known, you may find helpful

information written about them in business guides, newspapers, chamber of commerce publications, and other public documents. You may be able to obtain basic biographies by simply telephoning their office. A little imagination can yield impressive results. But the most valuable information you need to obtain should include personality traits that can affect interpersonal contact or environmental factors pertaining to a specific negotiation. Is your opponent vain? Do you have common enemies? Is he impatient? Does he possess an explosive temper? Does he lack integrity? Is he overly concerned with his image and reputation? What are his prejudices? What are his foibles? What are his habits? What does he fear? Answers to these questions (and more) will assist any negotiator in dealing with an opponent.

At times it can be difficult to obtain information from an opponent, depending on the situation and the type of information desired. Some opponents are more forthcoming than others. If you want to obtain the most difficult information prepare a list of known items first. For example, as a former investigator, I knew that in the interview (a form of negotiation) with a suspect, I would likely learn little from the suspect, unless that person had already decided to confess. In all but the rarest cases suspects must be convinced to confess. The way to convince them to confess, if you don't possess all the evidence, is to persuade them to give it to you. Preparation is the key. Investigators gather as much information as possible, through other sources, and prepare a list of facts to use in the interview. The list includes unknowns which if learned could secure a conviction against the suspect. Seasoned investigators ask questions that they already know the answers to and check if the suspects responses are truthful. If the suspect lies, the investigator points out that he has confirmed otherwise and asks the person to provide a truthful response. It is important to have the other person actually say the truth rather than tell him what you suspect and ask him to confirm it. Convince him to actually describe it in his own words. Once he begins telling the truth he will usually reveal more information than originally requested. Most negotiating opponents are honest and do not wish to be perceived to be lying. Resist correcting their false answer with the truth, just mention that you would like them to provide more accurate data and press until they do. Once they start offering truthful answers to the questions, slip in the questions you don't have the answers to and they will likely provide the truth. Then <u>confirm</u> it.

Obviously, business negotiations are not interrogations but if an opposing negotiator senses that you are well prepared he will likely provide a truthful response, when you pose that critical question, rather than appear untruthful. Your preparation must set the stage for the key questions you plan to pose at some point in the negotiation. Never boast about how knowledgeable you are or project the appearance that you do not trust the NP. Quite the opposite, you must emphasize that you trust him completely and would be disappointed if the NP violated that trust. Build an expectation of trust that the NP will want to live up to.

Know your negotiating style as well as your opponents. Most people have a pattern or habit that they follow even when it's not in their interest. Your personal weaknesses as well as those of your opponent can be manipulated to an advantage. Ask others who know the NP, or who have negotiated with him in the past, about his habits and weaknesses. Keep detailed records of them when possible. Review the notes before every negotiating session. Most negotiators acknowledge the importance of gathering intelligence on the NP but few actually follow through with it. Most excuse themselves by complaining they cannot devote the time to keep such files and records. On the other hand, what would a negotiator pay for such information when it's needed? Background and personality information about an NP can be priceless and it is not that difficult to gather.

B. GATHERING INTELLIGENCE

It always surprises me how many individuals volunteer negative information about their company or specific employees, to outsiders. Information about company problems, personality traits and weaknesses of key personnel, intra office fighting and a variety of other important data may be revealed in casual conversation. As a negotiator, wouldn't you like to know that your opponent has a high opinion of himself but has experienced a few recent failures and must return with a successful agreement on his next assignment or his job may be in jeopardy? These facts could be crucial in helping a negotiator exert leverage with that person at the negotiating table. Loyal employees are taught to keep such information "within the family" of the company, so to speak. If you meet a person who volunteers such information exploit it to the fullest and always protect the source. Koreans are not as free with negative information as Americans but can be prompted to provide delicate information if approached in the right environment, for example, at evening drinking get-togethers. Every organization has disgruntled employees who relish airing the dirty laundry of their company, but it is surprising the number of loyal employees who unwittingly do the same.

The following open sources are a few suggested places to begin the search for information about specific people and businesses depending on the size and importance of the entity or person:

Information about specific people and businesses

Who's Who
Dunn and Bradstreet Reports
Trade magazines
American Chamber of Commerce in Korea
Other Chambers of Commerce in Korea
Individual American businesses in Korea
The personal networks of your trusted employees
Newspaper files
✓ The U.S. Embassy
Competitors
Public documents
Annual Reports
Charitable organizations that person may belong to
Schools they attended

In Korea, everyone knows someone who knows about the person you are interested in. Social networks have long fingers in Korean society and with the right contacts you can find out anything. As the saying goes, there are no secrets in Korea.

In preparations for important negotiations, know the NP's area of expertise. Determine his level and limit of negotiating authority. Keep records of specialties, personal bios, professional history, assignments, education, travel, birthdays, anniversaries and other general information. This data will be helpful in establishing and maintaining relationships. Don't trust your memory. Write it down. Then use the information to your advantage.

Experienced negotiators also plan for what issues to avoid. These might include issues embarrassing for the company, embarrassing to the negotiator, or specific aspects of the deal that might make the NP uncomfortable. Prioritize what you want to accomplish and what you are prepared to concede. Prepare a script of what you expect to happen and in what sequence. Finally, prepare yourself. Open your mind. If you harbor any bias or prejudice about working in Asia or with Asians, clear the slate. Fill your mind with facts not rumors or stereotypes. Get ready to experience new things without rushing to form value judgements. Prepare yourself for stereotypes others may have of you. Think about how you will react to those situations calmly and professionally.

Protecting Yourself - Just as you are gathering valuable information on your opponents, expect the NP to gather information about you. Large Korean conglomerates are notorious for pursuing competitive intelligence and even industrial espionage. In November 1999 a survey conducted by the Korea Chamber of Commerce an Industry revealed that nearly 50% of business experienced some type of industrial espionage. Over 1,000 entities were surveyed including joint ventures, Korean firms and foreign firms operating in Korea.[1] One example that received considerable publicity occurred in February, 1998. South Korea Police arrested 16 engineers for industrial espionage against Samsung Electronics and LG Semicon. The men were believed to have been selling valuable information to a Taiwan based company.[2] Several of the suspects were former Samsung employees. A few of the most glaring examples have appeared in the newspapers but the South Korean National Intelligence Service, at one point, acknowledged industrial espionage within Korea as a serious problem. It is common for large Korean companies to operate a corporate intelligence unit. Every busi-

---

[1] Korea Herald, 50% of Firms Suffer Industrial Espionage: Survey, 11/24/99.

[2] Mark Carroll & David Lammers. "Taiwan DRAM Maker Linked to espionage in Korea." WWW.techweb.com/investor/INV199802S0006.

ness should train it's personnel to avoid conversation with outsiders about the company and it's employees. A strong defensive training program, should include methodology for identifying, reporting and tracking attempts by outsiders to gather information about your company. Such training, reinforced periodically, over time, can inoculate employees and prevent unwanted difficulties.

C. DEVELOP A STRATEGY

Developing strategy is a positive element of preparation. Like the football analogy mentioned before, professional teams have a game plan and stick with it. Few successful teams enter a game unprepared, they know what they want to accomplish and how they plan to accomplish it. Even though most teams have the ability to score on any single play coaches know they must employ a combination of plays that will move them incrementally closer to scoring a touchdown. Negotiators too must not try to win the game on one play. Especially in the Orient, complex negotiations will require time, and a team effort, to ultimately succeed. While every coach would be happy to win without allowing the other team to score, practical coaches expect to surrender a score along the way to final victory. Practical negotiators also expect their opponent to gain something in the process. Even the most legendary negotiators do not win everything while losing nothing. Be realistic in your expectations and plan to allow your opponent to win only those items that are the least important to you. Plan your opening, anticipate how the NP might respond, what difficult questions may arise, and how the negotiation will progress. Plan to test the NP's honesty along the way (see Testing for Honesty).

Plan to maintain a detailed journal of all negotiations so future NP's cannot distort the record. Memories fade rapidly and the journal will serve to settle possible arguments over what previously transpired. Substitute negotiators may need to refer to the records to quickly familiarize themselves with the negotiation.

Remember that preparation is not limited to the period before the negotiation begins. Preparation is needed in all phases of a negotiation. Throughout the proceedings, information must be gathered and recorded in case circumstances change. Plan all the way to the end of the negotiation. Planning should not cease until the negotiation has concluded. Then begin preparing for the next one.

Obviously, all records should be safeguarded for use in future negotiations when possible. It is not unusual to know well in advance that additional negotiations will be required. Contracts expire on schedule and must be re-negotiated, or opportunities may arise for additional work with the same company. It's best to assume there will be additional negotiations when gathering initial information and preparing for the first meeting.

Talk in terms of the other mans interests.

— Dale Carnegie

D. DETERMINE NEEDS OF BOTH SIDES

Both you and your NP have needs and they extend far beyond money. Don't forget the personal needs in the Maslow hierarchy such as safety, security, belonging and self-actualization — all NP's have them.

By identifying the NP's needs you can better search for a method to satisfy both sides and conclude a successful negotiation. This is as true in everyday life situations as it is in business negotiations. For example, before negotiating with a landlord for an apartment in Seoul I took the time to prepare for our first meeting. First, I met a mutual friend who gave me some highly valuable information. He mentioned that the landlord was financially well off and money was not his major concern. The landlord maintained the apartment with the intent of eventually giving it to his son a few years later. He merely wanted a reliable tenant to live in the apartment and take care of it in the interim. The previous tenant had literally destroyed the apartment and kept it so dirty the landlord decided not to renew the lease. The apartment was in a convenient location and had been attractive at one time. I was off to a solid start but still needed more information. I dropped by the apartment with my family, and took the time to talk with the security guard. I tried my best to make a favorable impression which I hoped would be passed on to the landlord. The security guard told me about personal differences the previous tenant had with the landlord. I visited the complex administration office and was told by the apartment authorities the actual worth of the specific apartment and they informed me of what price other similar apartments in the building were renting for. When I finally met the landlord, I did my best to look and act like the perfect tenant. I promised to take care of his apartment and return it to him in a condition he would be pleased with. I agreed to periodic inspection by him if he desired. He admitted he had talked with the security guard and received favorable comments about our family. I sensed I was just the tenant he was looking for. When I explained my only problem was that the rent was a little too high he eagerly agreed to my price. In addition, he completely remodeled the inside and later purchased all the wallpaper and decorations we chose. The short preparation for that negotiation saved me a large sum of money and allowed me to live quite happily in an apartment I otherwise could not have afforded.

E. Controlling the Agenda

In business as in diplomacy, the agenda represents an opportunity to gain and hold the initiative.[3] The order and specific topics of discussion can be two of the most important aspects of the negotiation. It is so important in fact, that depending on your opponent, a struggle may develop to actually control the agenda. It may be impossible for you to totally control the agenda but it is critical that you do not lose control of it. The agenda may become an area for concessions on either side so consider it in your strategy.

Setting the agenda should be an integral part of negotiation planning. The agenda frames the actual negotiation so list the items, time frames, and exact order you wish to proceed. It is said, people are fools for the written word. The written agenda has a powerful effect on all participants. An agenda can be a revealing document, most often it provides some insight into what is important to the NP. In formal negotiations, it's smart to confirm the agenda before talks begin. Ensure the individual points on the agenda, as well as the order and time allotted for each are to your satisfaction. Korean NP's may seek to alter the agenda after negotiations begin if they were not able to obtain

---

[3] Chester L. Karass, *Give and Take: The Complete Guide to Negotiating Strategies and Tactics*, (New York: Thomas Y. Crowell Publishers.) p. 5.

what they originally sought. Use their requests for changes as an opportunity to receive concessions in other areas. Agree to changes only if they agree to concede to something in return.

Disagreements over agendas can generate deadlock even before a negotiation begins. In November of 1999, talks between South Korea and the U.S. were stalled by disagreement over how to proceed with negotiations. Two issues were to be discussed; technical matters pertaining to the 300km range missiles and Korea's request for the U.S. to recognize it's plan to develop 500km missiles. The Korean side wished to negotiate the matters separately while the U.S. demanded to negotiate the issues simultaneously.[4] Talks were deadlocked until this basic agenda item could be resolved.

The deliberations to prepare for the historic North-South Summit in April-May of 2000 were mostly about agenda. As late as May 8th, the two sides disagreed on agenda items including the size of the press corps to cover the event.[5] After a more than month of discussion, the both sides finally approved an agenda.

As Chester Karrass reminds us. *"The person who controls the agenda controls what will be said and, perhaps more important, what will not be said."* [6]

Clarifying and controlling the agenda should be a priority in all preparations for international negotiations.

---

[4] Korea Herald. "Missile Talks Deadlocked because of Differences in Negotiating Procedure." WWW. Koreaherald.co.kr/1999/11/02/99.

[5] Seok, Kyong-hwa, "Koreans Hold Talks on Summit Agenda." The Associated Press, 8 May. 2000.

[6] Chester L. Karass, *Give and Take: The Complete Guide to Negotiation Strategies and Tactics*, (New York: Thomas Y. Crowell Publishers, 1974.) p. 5.

CHAPTER 4

Understanding Each
Others Culture

CHAPTER 4 Understanding Each Others Culture

Americans often mistakenly believe all cultures are basically the same, that American customs and behaviors are universal. Especially in the case of Korea, nothing could be further from the truth. I have written before that Korean culture is not just different from American culture, in many ways, it is opposite. Koreans appear to have an attraction/revulsion to foreigners and things foreign. As Korea modernized the people developed a profound interest for foreign ideas, products and culture. This is evidenced by the penetrating influence of foreign culture in their society. At the same time, they possess a strong pride and are deeply nationalistic, resenting foreigners and things foreign. This love/hate relationship can be a minefield for foreigners conducting business or negotiating with Koreans. Foreigners must delicately determine which parts of American culture are acceptable and which parts are disliked by their Korean counterpart.

The following concepts, both American and Korean, effect intercultural negotiations. The concepts listed are not all inclusive but were selected for their illustrative ability in highlighting differences in culture.

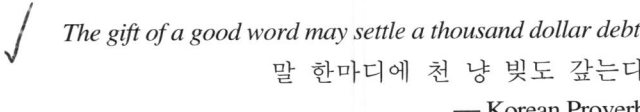

The gift of a good word may settle a thousand dollar debt.
말 한마디에 천 냥 빚도 갚는다
— Korean Proverb

A. Gibun

Americans often disregard this important concept. But accept it or not *Gibun* is an integral part of the Korean psyche. In short, *Gibun* is the essence of the Korean spirit. Some describe it is a combination of self-esteem, mood, feelings, and a person's inner spirit. Recognizing it's mere existence, however, is not quite as important as understanding it's care and well-being. Maintaining harmony is of great significance in maintaining a healthy *gibun*. If your NP's *gibun* is well, he may more readily accept your proposals. Of course to disturb the NP's *gibun* with negatives, especially if presented abruptly, could destroy the negotiation. In general, Koreans hesitate to introduce negatives directly, and are reluctant to present unpleasant news, or say "no" abruptly. They are also hesitant to relay bad news to elders, especially in the early morning, for fear of ruining that person's *gibun* for the entire day. Foreigners should consider these courtesies when dealing with Korean NPs, especially when discussing major issues of significant impact. A foreigner's approach and ability to smoothly relate negative information, can significantly effect how Koreans react, to the specific issue, and how they remember that person long afterward. While negatively affecting one's *gibun* is unwise, positively influencing it is certainly welcomed and encouraged. The foreigner who strives to pump the NP's *gibun*, making them happy even in times of difficulty, is on the road to close cooperation and success. The actual method of pumping one's *gibun* is considerably more complicated than mere flattery. It's a combination of making a person feel comfortable, relaxed, unthreatened and happy all at once. To successfully accomplish this, avoid situations that may even slightly embarrass, be flexible enough to overlook slight mistakes, especially in English language usage, and keep a cheery disposition at all times. Allow the NP to discuss matters of his own interest and respond favorably throughout the conversation. This really isn't difficult as Koreans are amicable guests, hosts and business negotiators. However, little things foreigners sometimes do, often without realizing, can quickly spoil a pleasant mood. Take special care in wording negative comments or replies. Koreans generally take notice of and appreciate a foreigner with tact. Westerners are frequently more comfortable providing completely open and honest answers to questions while Koreans prefer a more indirect approach which considers the feelings of others. It might be argued that Americans provide more bluntly honest feedback expecting the other person to be "thick skinned" and capable of accepting the truth. Koreans tend to provide indirect feedback assuming the other person's skin is "thin" and attempt to avoid inflicting any emotional pain on them. Foreigners who demonstrate the extra effort to respect Korean custom will be viewed as on attractive partner in Korean eyes and someone they will rush to develop a relationship and conduct business with. Sensing gibun is critical to fostering and maintaining the necessary harmony. The Westerner who works to develop skills and sensitivities to another's *gibun* will be on the path to stronger and more productive relationships.

B. PERSONAL SPACE

A very interesting concept quite different from the Western version, the Korean concept of space is sometimes the source of frustration and misunderstanding among foreigners. It may help to first examine the American concept for comparison with

Conceptions of Personal Space

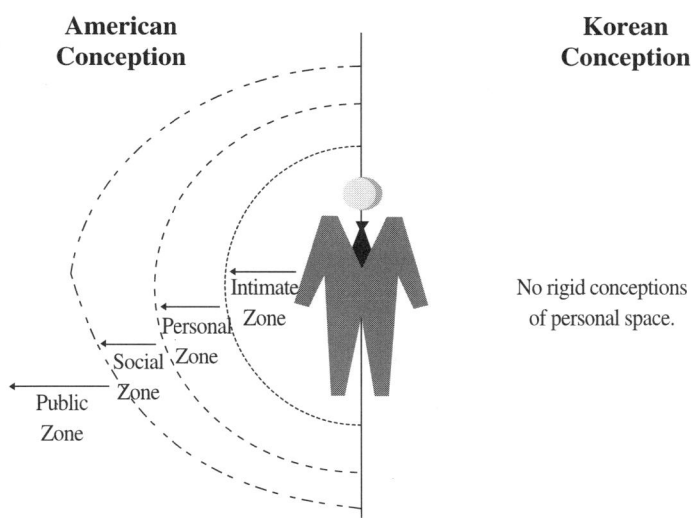

American Conception

Korean Conception

Intimate Zone
Personal Zone
Social Zone
Public Zone

No rigid conceptions of personal space.

the Korean. In the 1960's, one researcher (Edward T. Hall, 1966) studied American personal space and discovered a four-tier system of interpersonal distances. The first, from about 0 to 1/2 feet, he labeled an intimate zone; from 1/2 to 4 feet, a personal zone, from 4 to 12 feet, a social zone and over 12 feet was labeled a public zone. While the distances may vary slightly, as a group, Americans are sensitive about the boundaries of these zones and become uncomfortable when others ignore them. For example, in America, if one person enters another's intimate zone, for conversation, the person may find the other retreating to add the proper distance. Invading intimate space may be used to show confrontation, as when people are arguing, or it may show confidentiality, like when someone is whispering in your ear. In both America and Korea, confidentiality whispering is usually done from the front or side, not from the rear, which would show some romantic intentions.

If a person brushes or bumps another, even in a crowded area, in effect they invaded that person's intimate space and American culture requires that a person acknowledge and apologize for such an act by begging pardon or saying "excuse me." Ironically, Americans are somewhat more territorial and often lay claim to space even temporarily. For example, anyone who has ever attended a class or briefing without assigned seating may have noticed that after a break, most people return to the same seat and become offended if someone occupies that space even though other equal open spaces are available. Koreans, on the other hand, live in one of the most densely populated countries in the world and haven't had the luxury of large individual spaces. They frequently bump into each other on crowded streets, subways, buses and markets, and are forced to routinely share precious space with others. They normally don't apologize for straying too close to one another, in these situations, because within their culture, they have committed no violation. Often foreigners visit Korean markets or crowded streets and remark how rude or pushy Koreans are for jostling or bumping into them without apology. This may be a result of not understanding different notions of space.

The issue of touching, in general, is also different between East and West. Some foreigners may be surprised to see Korean members of the same sex, both male and female, holding hands or walking with their arms around another's shoulder, without any sexual connotation. This type of behavior is normal between close friends. Among men, foreigners may be surprised to find a Korean friend clasp his hand when meeting or place his hand on the foreigner's leg during a drinking party or friendly discussion. Again, this is not a sexual advance but a simple gesture among friends. This can be somewhat unnerving for a foreigner unaware of this behavior and may still be difficult to become comfortable with even after learning of it. Conversely, a few American customs involving touch, like the slap on the back, or the gentle punch in the arm, are considered quite rude by Koreans.

Office space provides a glimpse at another cultural contrast. As might be expected from an individual centered culture, it is normal to expect individual offices in Western society. In fact, office size is often an indicator of status and position. Even if offices are not completely walled they are frequently separated by partitions and individually decorated. It is common to see diplomas, family pictures, and others items displayed to personalize that particular space. Koreans are more likely to encourage open offices with desks grouped together and aligned so the supervisor may view the subordinates. Individual office spaces are more rare and reserved for high-ranking positions in Korea, although recently more large businesses use partitioned space in a limited sense.

Foreigners tend to view Koreans through the spacial rules of their own culture instead of the rules of their hosts. Understanding the differences associated with this complex concept may help promote better understanding between the different cultures.

C. NAMES - DIFFERENT THAN YOU MAY BE USED TO

While it may seem basic, foreign negotiators are often ensnared by fundamental cultural difference in Korea. However, details can often mean the difference in success. Names are one of those small but important details that can make encounters uncomfortable if not handled properly. In the Orient, custom dictates that personal names are written in order of family name, first name and middle name, and with few exceptions names will contain three syllables. So the name Kim Woo-Choong refers to Mr. Kim. It may appear written in English in a couple of variations including a comma after the family name but the most common and easily understood form is the one as written above with a hyphen between the given and middle names. Confusion may result when meeting Koreans who deal frequently with Westerners or have lived abroad. A number of them have adopted the Western custom of writing names with the given name first, and so in the example above, it's possible to receive a business card that says Woo-Choong Kim. If meeting for the first time a foreigner might mistakenly think he is Mr. Woo. Don't worry though as this is by far the exception. Take care to learn the name correct early as it is embarrassing to mistake a name.

While it may not be readily apparent, a number of Korean names take on different looks when translated into English. Names such as Lee, Rhee, Yi, Yee, Li, all come from the same Korean derivative pronounced more like "EE". Koreans often try to spell their name in English in such a way as to make it easier for foreigners to pronounce it correctly. As a result Pak becomes Park, to preclude pronunciation as "pack". EE becomes Lee because it is unusual for Americans to encounter a name without consonants.

It won't take long to discover there are an extraordinary number of Kim's, Lee's and Pak's in this country. Astoundingly, the three names combined constitute about 43% of the population broken down as Kim 21%, Lee 14.8%, and Pak 8.5%. Of course these three names are a small portion of the total family names in existence. In all, there are well over 150 other names including fairly common ones such as Choi, Chung, Shin, Im, Paek, Kang, and Chang etc.

Remember that names are personal to Koreans and are usually not used in conversation Westerners generally feel more comfortable using first names and often consider it a sign of friendship. Westerners may be tempted to develop a "first name basis" with Korean business contacts to feel secure in the relationship. DO NOT practice this in Korea. First names are rarely used and most often only between the closest friends in certain circumstances. Position names or titles are more common and are used in place of personal names (director, doctor, general, uncle, etc.). Most positions maintain a corresponding title that may be used in conversation. Even family members have terms to label their relative positions such as oldest brother, younger sister, cousin etc., and individuals will be likely referred to by this label, as opposed to their given names. Even in marriage, names are rarely used between spouses, substituting a nickname or such to call each other. When conversing with unfamiliar persons the word teacher, pronounced *Seon Saeng Nim,* is a kind of cover-all reference, especially when speaking to an elder, as it acknowledges respect for the person's age and status. A teacher in Korea, occupies a respected position and is given special deference within the language. The title, teacher, can also be used in conjunction with a family name, for example, Lee *Seon Saeng Nim.*

During conversation don't be afraid to omit a name altogether. Actually, with a little practice, people can easily converse without referring to each other by name. This is the safest method especially if the two are not familiar with each other or are unsure of one another's position or title. If this is too difficult to master, try using a position title and last name only like, Director Kim, Doctor Lee, etc., but never just the last name, for example "Hey Kim", as it is considered rude and can quickly spoil a relationship. In general, a foreigner can safely use the term Mister, combined with a last name, but when meeting persons of much higher rank, Mister Kim, for example, may not signify enough respect and might be considered impolite. In Western culture, when meeting a President, Ambassador, Senator, Judge etc., it is preferable to address them as Judge Jones rather than Mr. Jones. The same courtesy applies in Korea, but to an even greater degree.

Also remember that the rule for Mister does not apply to Mrs. Women retain their maiden name after marriage so Mr. Kim's wife is not Mrs. Kim. She is normally referred to as the wife of Mr. Kim (there are specific Korean terms for it). The terms vary and become more significant if the woman is the boss's wife, the preachers wife, or the wife of a high ranking individual. Before becoming frustrated or discouraged by the complexity, remember foreigners are relatively safe not referring to wives at all by name, but speaking as described above. If a foreigner is unsure, but wants to show proper respect, it is always acceptable to use the term teacher as explained above. It is generally acceptable to use Miss when addressing unmarried women although there is a specific term for them in Korean (*Agassi*).

Another short tip, never write a persons name in red. It is reserved for the dead and considered impolite.

In negotiation, referring to the NP properly can help prevent unnecessary animosity. Take the time to learn the NP's name and title and to use it properly.

D. FACE

As *gibun* is a reflection of the inner spirit so face is the essence of one's outward image. This concept is found in both Western and Oriental cultures, in one form or another, and includes both individual social and professional reputation. The concept of face is readily associated with Asian culture. However, although often disguised and not easily recognizable, face, in various forms, is certainly part of Western tradition also. Westerners attempt to spare another's feelings or protect a reputation by employing means such as "giving the person an out" or "throwing a bone" to someone who is about to experience a loss. Westerners may not readily recognize it as such, but in essence it's done to protect a person's outward image or "face." In the Orient, the emphasis and importance, of this outward image, are magnified in comparison to the West. Maintaining or saving face is vital when dealing with Koreans in any type of social or business setting. Be sensitive to actions that might cause them to lose face. As such, avoid situations that could publicly embarrass or cause them feel uncomfortable, when possible.

In negotiations, it's wise to compromise, at certain times, to allow a Korean partner to save face or maintain a respectable image. Allowing him to lose face could result in a tactical victory but possibly a devastating strategic loss. Koreans may spend well beyond their means to entertain, form a favorable impression, or fulfill an obligation. Again, this is often done to save face. Pardon me if I dare quote a Japanese Emperor to illustrate how Koreans feel about this principal: "To lose face is everything, but to lose everything is not necessarily to lose face." Somewhat exaggerated but it makes a point.

Remember that when presented with an embarrassing situation or one where a foolish mistake was made, Koreans often smile. The smile does not indicate a lack of regard for the mistake, it's their way of trying to smooth over the public embarrassment from it. This is at times confusing to Westerners, but face is largely responsible for this Korean reaction.

Recognizing the importance of face and dealing with it appropriately can save time and money, overcome resistance, and prevent unnecessary interpersonal difficulties.

Allowing an NP to save face in a negotiation may be the deal clincher. Never try to totally defeat your NP unless you are confident you will never negotiate in Korea again. A humiliated enemy is a formidable one.

At times, Americans will sacrifice harmony for honesty. For example, if presented with a first proposal and asked for a critique, an American might provide a sincere criticism offering honest opinions. This would almost certainly disrupt the harmony between the two people. Koreans, on the other hand, would probably mention the positive points and avoid direct criticism. Resist the temptation to offer criticism even when asked. Emphasize positives and avoid negative opinions whenever possible.

In some forms Americans do not respect face saving and even view it as a weakness. Americans intuitively respect thick-skinned people who confront problems squarely. Although Americans practice a form of face saving they don't like it, and use it infrequently.

Koreans are reluctant to admit they do not know and usually will not admit it readily. Americans are also reluctant to admit they do not know but in the end will admit it. No shame or stigma is attached to saying I don't know for Americans as long as they promise to find out and report back later. But for

Koreans, not knowing is often too embarrassing to admit and so they sometimes provide an answer to save face. This can be disconcerting and Americans should be careful to determine when the NP may be providing an answer you wish to hear just to save face.

E. DIFFERENCES IN COMMUNICATING (WHEN NOT TO TAKE YES FOR AN ANSWER)

Direct vs Indirect Communication — Americans believe in direct communication. American philosophy demands that we identify problems and confront them. We respect those who function in the same way. Koreans value indirect communication in order to save face and preserve harmony. In general, Americans are direct communicators, who believe in blunt honesty and who respect those who are tough enough to face difficulties directly. The English language is full of expressions illustrating this point; for example, Let's stop beating around the bush, what's the bottom line, let's get right to the point, just say what you mean, or give it to me straight, to name just a few. Koreans are indirect communicators. Because of their concern for the other persons' feelings they are more circumspect in their expression. They truly appreciate someone who can refrain from directly exposing negative points, especially those that might embarrass another person. Americans respect an ability to cut straight to the point regardless of where the chips may fall. But, to Koreans, this often appears as inconsideration toward the feeling of others. Americans should consider the necessity of employing tact when dealing with Korean NP's. Of course, by our cultural standard Americans are not inconsiderate in this regard and often try to acknowledge the feelings of others by prefacing tough talk with phrases like "I hope you will understand" or "I'm sorry to have to say this." In the context of Korean culture this would not be an acceptable effort and could still generate i'll feelings. Although, showing more sensitivity to your NP's cultural norms may seem to take more time, in the long run it may build the type of relationship that will actually quicken agreement, clinch a deal or allow resolution to a problem.

Americans generally prefer learning of bad news or potential problems as soon as possible. Koreans respect timing bad news to preserve harmony and decorum. So Americans should communicate a negative answer in the most indirect way possible.

F. THE LOGIC OF THE DEAL VS STRENGTH OF RELATIONSHIP

Americans place the highest importance on the details of the agreement. Americans believe that if the concept is logical and backed by sound analysis and data, the other side will surely recognize the benefit and quickly reach an agreement. In general, Americans tend to mitigate the importance of the relationship between the parties of the deal. In fact, there are instances when Americans would agree that they could strike a deal with a partner they absolutely despise. As a result they spend far less time cultivating and nurturing relationships which often causes them great difficulty in negotiating with Koreans. Koreans view the relationship as the most important aspect of the deal. In fact, there are times when Koreans will agree to a so-called bad deal just to preserve a relationship. And there are times when Koreans would refuse an attractive proposal for lack of relationship. This can be puzzling to Americans and they may leave a negotiation scratching their heads as to why the Korean NP would not reach to an agreement. By now you can see how the opposite philosophies of the two cultures can affect negotiations.

This paradox of philosophies extends to social relationships. Koreans depend on friends to assist them in situations that might even place the friend in jeopardy. Americans expect friends to protect them from situations that could put them in jeopardy. A hypothetical example may help illustrate. A Korean who committed a serious crime may confide in his friend and can expect the friend not to inform authorities. An American who committed a serious crime is expected not to inform his friend to prevent putting the friend in a situation where it is difficult to do his civic duty — inform the police. These are two considerably different relationship philosophies.

G. DISPARITY IN KNOWLEDGE OF FOREIGN LANGUAGE AND CULTURE

This is a stereotype that may be closest to the truth. In general, Americans are ignorant of Korean culture and language. Given that Korean is a difficult language and the culture is, in a variety of ways, quite different from our own, Americans tend to excuse themselves for the inadequacy. However, those who plan to spend any time in Korea especially in business or government, should devote at least a portion of their time to learning the culture and basics of the Korean language. To do so creates great advantages at little cost, while failure to do so may result in unnecessary difficulties that may be ruinous. Ironically, the basics of Korean are easily acquired. The 24 letter alphabet can be mastered in a day. While learning the intricacies of grammar are more difficult, it is well worth the effort for negotiators to learn the rudiments of spoken and written Korean.

H. FAIRNESS

This concept of fairness is part of the American psyche. Unlike other cultures, the American brand of fairness not only insists on fair treatment for "me" but also demands a square deal for "you." This is a great concept if both sides abide by this cultural norm. When negotiating internationally, you will find other cultures have different concepts of fairness and the American form can be an exploitable weakness. The idea of being fair is so strong that it reaches even into the relationship of warring parties. In his book "In the Eye of the Storm" General Norman Schwarzkoph admitted he was "suckered" during critical negotiations with the Iraqis following the Gulf War. During the war, Schwarzkoph had referred to the Iraqi Army as "a marauding band of armed looters in uniform." He had described them as a bunch of rapists and thugs. After the war, the triumphant general met with Iraqi generals in Safwan, in southern Iraq, to negotiate the terms for ending the Gulf War. He was clearly in the superior negotiating position. He could have demanded almost anything from the Iraqis and could have denied almost any Iraqi request. His main goals were to secure the swift transfer of POWs and arrange procedures to prevent inadvertent fighting between coalition and Iraqi forces in the future. Schwarzkoph achieved those two goals quickly. Then the Iraqis made a few requests of their own. First, the Iraqis requested to be able to continue flying their helicopters. They explained that the coalition had destroyed most of the roads, bridges and the transportation system, and they needed to be able to transport government officials and prisoners around the country. Schwarzkoph felt the request was reasonable and agreed. Then they requested they be allowed to fly their aircraft armed, ostensibly for self protection, and the general agreed again. Later, the helicopters were actually used in putting down insurrections within Iraq, and other offensive moves by Saddam Hussein. General Schwarzkoph could have literally dictated the terms he wanted but he did not. I suggest the reason he didn't was his American desire to be fair and reasonable.

My intention is not to malign a hero of the Gulf War, but to make the key point that our cultural desire to be fair can produce results not necessarily in our interest. Savvy international negotiators know that when dealing with Americans, an appeal to our sense of fairness can win valuable concessions. Our desire to be fair is a proud part of our culture but we must use it wisely and not allow it to be used against us.

We have discussed win-win negotiations and they are generally desirable. However, all so called win-win negotiations are not to your advantage. Be careful what the other side wins. Let's go back and recognize the bold negotiating skills of the Iraqis. Iraq was an army totally defeated, in many ways humiliated, in one of the shortest wars of it's kind. The Iraqis, however, did not come to the table humbled. Schwarzkoph could have (and some say should have) demanded that the Iraqis surrender their military and war making equipment or face total destruction. Instead, they negotiated not only to keep certain aircraft, but to fly them armed. To add to their negotiated victory consider this. Schwarzkoph, had, at one time, issued an order that anything flying over Iraq would be shot down. So in effect, the Iraqis were able to retain and fly their helicopters and negotiate an exception to the no fly rule. This should go down in history as a brilliant and gutsy negotiation move.

Fairness also inhibits Americans from using techniques that would be to our advantage in negotiation. For example, professional negotiators recommend making high initial demands to draw out the NP's position and allow more flexibility in negotiating range. However, Americans are often reluctant to submit unusually high demands for fear they would appear unreasonable and unfair. Dr. Herbert Goldhamer described how the American reluctance to present such demands handicapped UN negotiation during the Korean Armistice negotiation.[1] The UN negotiators intended to demand a truce line north of the battle line and far north of the 38th parallel. They were reluctant and argued among themselves as to whether such a demand was morally justified. UN negotiators finally assembled a moral justification in their mind but Goldhamer suggested such a justification was not needed. Goldhamer wrote, I tended to treat this problem rather casually at first, indicating that I thought it was a useful argument to use but at the same time making it quite clear that I did particularly see that one needed such a justification for trying to get an advanced demarcation line. I indicated that of course one ought to get absolutely everything one could get within the limits of the costs that would have to be born by the UN in order to secure it's settlement with the Communists.[2] The belief that one should or could only ask for those things which were ethically justified was quite strong

---

[1] Dr. Herbert Goldhamer was an observer to the Ameristice negotiations between the UN and representatives of North Korea and China. His observations experiences were recorded in a text published by Rand Corporation.

[2] Herbert Goldhamer. *The 1951 Korean Armistice: A Personal Memoir*, (Santa Monica, Ca. Rand, 1994) p. 66.

[3] Ibid. p. 67.

when I arrived. The notion of getting what you can get was an idea that when I first expressed it in the camp was reacted to with some degree of shock.[3] The cultural imperative of acting morally in negotiation is not shared by all other nations. This imperative is so strong that when Americans perceive they are not being quite fair they often generate guilt. The guilt itself may result in concessions to attempt to compensate for previous treatment. This entire concept of fairness/guilt can be a striking disadvantage if the opposing side uses it to their advantage.

I. COMPETITION

Win/lose interactions are part of the competitive grain of American culture. Americans are taught, from an early age, to play to win, there are winners and losers, winning is every-thing, and nobody likes a loser. Americans create competitions out of even the most mundane aspects of life. In our dominat-ing sports culture, win/lose is emphasized to the point of fanaticism. So it is only natural for Americans to approach negotiation in the spirit of competition. Now I am not saying competition in itself is undesirable, as an American raised with the competitive spirit, I am inclined to defend it as part of America's strength. In inter-cultural negotiations however, more often than not, it may not produce the most favorable out-come. It is even difficult for some Americans to imagine that there are games where there can be more than one winner. On it's face it seems un-American, it would be like awarding all 1st place prizes at a track meet. But the truth is, negotiation need not be a competition, but a mutually beneficial association searching for ways to satisfy both sides. Koreans may be consid-ered the most competitive of Asians but in this category they cannot compare with Americans. So diffusing your own com-petitive spirit, even a little, may be the key to achieving a win/win negotiation.

Americans define themselves by their work. When meeting a person for the first time, our first question is often what do you do? We are a doing people, we define ourselves by our individual accomplishments. Koreans are more being people, defining themselves by who they are. Where they were born, what school they attended, and what family they are from, are all of importance to Koreans.

J. VERTICAL VS HORIZONTAL RELATIONSHIPS

Americans pride themselves on egalitarian social behavior. We like to treat everyone as relatively equal in the overall acheme of society. Korean society is ordered in a more vertical fashion with each individual occupying a place in the hierarchy. Individuals may move up or down in the hierarchy but they occupy a certain position based on factors such as age, experience, wealth and others. Where this concept becomes relevant to negotiation is in decision-making. In larger Korean companies, decisions are more likely reserved for top management. The individual Korean actually negotiating may have less latitude to make certain concessions than you may expect. In general, the American negotiator is more likely to be afforded additional authority to negotiate. Of course, this limitation can work to the Korean NP's advantage as he may be able to fend off requests for concessions by claiming the need to appeal to higher authority. Don't confuse authority with responsibility. Large companies may delegate the negotiation to a lower level of management while maintaining the commensurate level of authority at the executive level of the company. Be prepared for this possibility. Learn the NP's level and limits of authority as soon as possible, even before the negotiation begins.

K. GESTURES AND BODY LANGUAGE

Koreans instinctively know through culture what we go to college to learn, that 65% of all personal communication is non-verbal. In the book Body Language and Social Order, the author rightly points out that because we all speak English in America we think we understand each other. The truth is America contains a variety of subcultures with different non-verbal cues. Even between Americans there is misunderstanding. Imagine how much more difficult it must be for Koreans to understand Americans. Be certain you are sending the correct message with your non-verbals. It is quite possible the Korean NP is receiving a message different than you intended.

Eye contact is an important indicator of trust for Americans. It can also invite intimacy, especially if accompanied by other cues such as a smile or cocked head. Koreans consider continuous eye contact as somewhat impolite. Americans are reluctant to trust someone who fails to look them in the eye. It is acceptable to make periodical eye contact with your Korean NP to indicate interest.

Pointing is rude in both cultures and such behavior is rude both when executed with the index finger or with the thumb. A more polite gesture in both cultures is performed with the open hand and slightly outstretched arm.

Some cultures practice kissing on the cheek when greeting in public. This is performed without pelvic contact except for intimate encounters. Koreans are not comfortable with this type of behavior in any form.

Americans are usually more animated than Koreans when negotiating. It is not uncommon to see Americans making a variety of gestures, during meetings, that provide clues to their thoughts. For example, to see a person covering his eyes, or stroking his eyebrows, may indicate he secretly has difficulty accepting what the speaker is saying. A person looking down while picking imaginary lint off their pants may indicate quiet disapproval or disinterest. Have you ever done these things or observed another person do them? Chances are your Korean NP will sit almost expressionless through a negotiation. Remember, while he may not be revealing many non-verbal cues he certainly will be picking up cues from your behavior. Be careful that your non-verbal signals are not revealing unintended messages.

A few gestures are more universal. In both cultures, leaning forward often shows interest. The smile signals a person is approachable. It is universally understood. I have even tested this in airports where peddlers are trying to snag passers-by for money or engage them in conversation. I am usually avoided if I give the non-smile unapproachable look. Koreans are often expressionless or expression neutral so Americans may mistake that as unapproachable. However, it is not the case. Koreans are exceptionally friendly towards foreigners if approached properly within their cultural context.

The importance of meeting the NP should be self-evident. Even though there are instances when it is more advantageous to negotiate on the telephone, it is usually to your advantage to negotiate in person. While negotiating, remain alert for nonverbal cues from the NP as well as the cues you are sending to your opponent.

Common Negotiating Tactics/Techniques (and counters)

CHAPTER 5 Common Negotiating Tactics/Techniques (and Counters)

Each negotiation is a different situation so every negotiation requires a slightly different approach. Below are some of the most common tactics used by amateurs and professionals alike. You may already use modified combinations of these tactics or have had them used against you.

A. PUT YOURSELF ON THE SAME SIDE AS OPPONENT

Placing yourself and the opponent on the same side and posing the problem as the enemy, is the most positive of the negotiating techniques. The most successful negotiation is not a contest but a cooperative effort. This technique can be extremely effective. I like to use the simple example of negotiating for an extension on a library book. I will provide two scenarios, the first is the negotiation gone wrong, the second is the same situation as it actually happened. A man walks into the local library to pick up a book he ordered through an interlibrary loan. The librarian gives him the book and reminds him that this book must be returned in seven days instead of the customary two weeks. He replies, "don't you know it's impossible to read a book this thick in seven days." I have a job and other responsibilities and there is no way I can finish it in one week, he says disgustedly. The librarian stiffens and says "I'm sorry sir, rules are rules. This book was borrowed from another library and we must abide by their regulations. Seven days is the maximum." In this example the man placed himself at odds with both the librarian and the rules. The outcome was certainly predictable.

Now let's look at what really happened when he positioned himself on the same side as the librarian. When the librarian gave him the book and informed him of the seven day requirement he actually said with a smile. "Gee, the contents of this book are quite important to me and it is rather thick. Im afraid I will need it longer than a week." Rules are rules, she said. We must follow the loaning library's regulations on inter library loans. He said, "I know you have been a librarian for some time. I know the importance of the rules and I certainly would not want to violate them. I imagine you are empathetic to those of us who like to read. With all your experience in these matters what would you suggest that might help solve this dilemma?" Well, she said, we don't do it often but if I called over to the library and asked, they might grant an extension." I certainly would appreciate it, he said, again with another smile. Within a few minutes he got the extension. This simple example illustrates three points; it reinforces the, everything is negotiable, statement I made earlier, it illustrates the importance of approaching at the proper time and in the proper manner, and most importantly it demonstrates the effectiveness of placing yourself on the same side as your opponent and maintaining the focus on the problem as the joint enemy. In this example, by positioning the rules as the enemy, and including the librarian in the solution, a win-win outcome was reached. The man (me) received what he wanted, (my extension) and the librarian, I'm sure, felt better about herself for helping resolve a problem.

In this case, what worked in America would be even more likely to succeed in Korea. Appealing to your Korean counterpart as a friend and competent professional, helping arrive at a solution together, will allow both sides to negotiate favorable results. Relationship is a critical component, coupled with courtesy, and the combination of both will result in a more positive resolution. Koreans are the ultimate realists. In general, they can be counted on to do what is in their interests. Frame the negotiation so it appeals to their interests as well as your own. When an NP says, I must have 10% raise to cover inflation, ask how you can work together to solve the NP's problem, and ask to discuss the details of the NP's situation. Mr. Ury advises to ask problem-solving questions like, I see you feel strongly about this could you help me understand it better.[1] This works well with Korean NP's. Avoid confrontation, use understanding. Attempt to discover the source of the problem.

B. MENTOR APPROACH

Ask the NP's advice. The Korean NP may feel a source of pride by advising his American counterpart. This approach works best when two parties are negotiating from a position of having worked together and are searching for reasons to continue a positive relationship. At times you may act as mentor. An example here may help understand my point. A Korean employee once came into my office to quit. When asked why, she said the job was too stressful and she couldn't handle it any-

---

[1] Roger Fisher and William Ury, *Getting to Yes, Negotiating Agreement without Giving In.* (Boston: Houghton Mifflin Company, 1981).

more. Since it was difficult to lose this stressed, but otherwise, good employee I probed for more answers. It turned out the highly conscientious employee had more assignments than she could complete to perfection. Being a perfectionist, this left her feeling extremely frustrated. After consulting with her direct supervisor to help her prioritize assignments and by establishing parameters of quality for each product, she was almost instantly turned back into a happy, productive and relaxed worker. By acting as the mentor and not the boss we were able to successfully forge a solution to the problem.

C. CO-OPT

Koreans are masters of hospitality. They are highly skilled at developing relationships and putting Americans at ease. Korean hospitality is quite enjoyable when given in traditional kindness but can be treacherous when performed by unscrupulous persons or with the intent of taking advantage. I have seen scores of employees, executives, investors and other trusting individuals taken advantage of under the guise of hospitality. The scenario unfolds like this. Unsuspecting executives arrive in Korea and are pampered by a Korean NP, business partner or fellow employee. They are smothered with kindness to influence the person to be more flexible and feel slightly obligated to the NP. Americans hate to admit they have been influenced like this but it happens more frequently than most people realize. Of course, most Korean hospitality is genuine and I encourage you to enjoy it. However, to maintain integrity and keep yourself in a safe negotiating position, attempt to control it or reciprocate the kind favors as much as possible.

D. FORCED DECISION

Will you decide right now? Sellers are trained to engage those with the authority and the commitment to buy. They often try to pressure customers into a decision or concession by asking a question like, If I offer the best deal are you prepared to decide to buy today? With this question they kill two birds with one stone. They immediately discover if you have the authority and commitment to buy or are just trifling. Secondly, they prepare you for the actual sales pitch.

COUNTER TECHNIQUE

When an NP questions your authority and you sense it is merely a tactic, question his authority and commitment to sell, which almost always catches him off guard. I remember a salesman that came out to assist me while examining the used cars on the lot. After a short talk he popped the big question. If I offer you a good deal will you buy this car right now, today? I countered by questioning him, If I make you an offer do you have the authority and commitment to sell this car right here without any side discussions with your sales manager? He was totally disarmed. He agreed to work with me according to my conditions and timetable.

NP's may try to force a decision by playing to an audience. People who use this tactic often believe they are anonymous while employing it. A high official I knew comes to mind when I think of this tactic. During discussions or negotiations he would look around the room at others, gauging their impression of his answer and using their head nodding agreements to pressure others to agree with him. One day I suggested moving the discussion to a more private place and the tactic stopped immediately.

COUNTER TECHNIQUE

Identify the technique without making the NP defensive. Offer a suggestion such as maybe we should move to a private place free of distractions. If you expose the technique too bluntly the NP may become defensive. A response like, I can see you are just playing to the audience, is likely to bring quick denials from an NP, and generate a hostile attitude toward you.

If the NP is trying to force a decision, and you would like time to think it over, it is appropriate to respond with something like, I really see we are close on this and I could give you a decision right now if you want me to, but the decision would be no. How about allowing me a few days (hours etc.) to think this over and get back to you.

E. DIVIDE AND CONQUER

The more complex the negotiation the more need to break it into smaller parts. Negotiators should maintain the principle of negotiating an entire package while simultaneously working to gain agreement on as many sub elements as possible. Begin by gaining agreement on the simplest issues. Break the negotiation into a series of small yeses. This will establish a positive negotiating atmosphere with the NP. Areas of deep disagreement are best saved for later discussion.

F. GOOD GUY/ BAD GUY

Also known as the Mutt and Jeff technique among policemen. In this technique, the good guy appeals to the soft side of the NP and tries to appear fair and reasonable. The bad guy is demanding, threatening and unreasonable. The good guy tries to convince the NP to work with him in order to avoid having to confront the bad guy. At times, the bad guy does not even have to exist. I have conducted negotiations where the bad guy was a fictitious boss. Once this approach backfired and I had to produce a boss. After that, I learned to be more careful in using a fictitious bad guy. In certain business situations you may introduce the bad guy as a higher authority. When Koreans use this technique the junior member will often be the bad guy and the senior member will play the good guy.

I remember an opponent who was so afraid of my bad guy that he agreed to let me negotiate on his behalf. Big mistake. He suggested, maybe you could talk to him for me, make him understand. Of course, no matter how strongly you trust the NP, never allow the opponent to be your chief advocate with his group. It is most likely a trap, and is certainly not to your advantage.

It is also wise to remember that Koreans may not want to enter a relationship that includes a bad guy so do not introduce this technique too early. It could cause the NP to decide that it is best to back out of the relationship entirely rather than deal with a bad guy lurking in the background.

COUNTER TECHNIQUE

If forced to deal with an actual bad guy, face to face, the most effective counter tactic is to let the bad guy wear himself out by ignoring him. Similarly, shutting out the bad guy may neutralize him, as Koreans want very much to feel included. You may try to shame the NP by placing the blame for spoiling the negotiation on the bad guy's negative attitude. If the NP's bad guy is real, force the NP's good guy to deal with his own bad guy. Tell him that the bad guy may ruin the deal and the good guy will lose face.

If the other sides bad guy is just an act, point out the tactic and ask them to stop it. You may also introduce your own bad guy to deal with NP's bad guy. At times two bad guys can cancel each other and the two good guys can work together more easily. If you are up to a real challenge try to turn around the bad guy by showing a little hospitality and kindness. A small percentage of bad guys can actually be made to act reasonably. In the end, refuse to accept the bad guy's tactics.

G. INNOCENT VICTIM

Appealing to an NP's sense of fairness, as a person, can be an effective negotiating tool. Certain types of negotiations better lend themselves to this approach, for example, negotiating for changes to a contract because of unexpected problems encountered after the negotiation originally concluded. Koreans are very understanding concerning these matters but they expect similar treatment from you during their hard times. Americans tend to be literalists and stick closely to the written contract, following every word precisely. Koreans are generally more flexible, making allowances due to unforeseen circumstances. The innocent victim technique works better against Americans but can also be effective with Koreans if they feel a sense of brotherhood towards you or your company.

H. DELAY

Also known as, Time Out. Koreans often need a delay to build consensus with different layers of management within their company. Expect at least some delays when dealing with Koreans and try not to show frustration. Instead, explore ways to obtain commitment on items not affected by delay. Maintain a pleasant attitude throughout. Delay may also be used to gracefully end a negotiation. Rather than conclude on a negative note, Koreans may delay, and you may do the same, using phrases like, I'd like time to think it over, Let me carefully consider this, or You make an interesting point let me consider it. Koreans may continuously delay to tire you out and force you to quit allowing them to deny any i'll will since you are the one who ended the relationship. A fake deadlock can also be a delay tactic. An NP may feign a deadlock to save face when he is caught unprepared. Try to determine the true intentions of the NP and work with him to resolve any obstacles blocking the negotiation.

I. HIGHER AUTHORITY

I have to ask my boss is one of the most common uses of this tactic. Everyone uses it, from a car salesman to a government official. Higher Authority can relieve pressure and prevent confrontation. A few experts suggest preparing a higher authority argument for later use in a negotiation because admitting you are the authority is a distinct disadvantage. If there is not a higher authority to yield to, then the NP could force you into a decision at a time not in your best interest. When negotiating in Korea, it's better to admit you have authority to negotiate to certain levels but there are circumstances that might require higher authority. This allows you to maintain a dignified status while reserving the higher authority for use if really needed.

This is the proper place to remind negotiators of the need to determine who actually has authority, back in the preparation phase. If the technique is used against you, the advantage will be yours if you know the actual line of authority.

COUNTER TECHNIQUE

If your intelligence says NP uses higher authority, defend against it by clarifying, in advance, who is the decision maker. Another defense is to claim the same difficulty and suggest a possible meeting between both higher authorities. Appeal to ego, secure the NP's commitment of support and obtain his approval before negotiating with higher authority. If NP actually introduces his higher authority, consider introducing yours as a counter.

J. TRADE-OFF

Too often we concede out of kindness which is quickly forgotten or totally unappreciated. Turn a concession into a positive gain for yourself. Anytime you give, ask for something in the same moment. "If we can do that for you what can you do for us." Or frame it as a polite question, If we do that can you help us with this?

Trading off can be an effective method in stopping the NP from continuously asking for concessions. Agreement to a trade off also implies a larger commitment to the overall proposal. When a Korean tailor told me I could not pick up a suit on Wednesday as he previously promised, I was a little disturbed. I didn't mind the one day delay as much as having to make the additional trip to his tailor shop. Instead of quickly agreeing or even arguing about his broken promise, I asked him to deliver the suit instead of forcing me to pick it up. He agreed to this concession which saved me a long drive and the one day delay was even less of an inconvenience. Another tailor who delayed my suit by several days, agreed to include a free shirt and two ties for the inconvenience. With Koreans, do not present a concession as a demand, for example, if I do that you will have to do this for me. Keep the concession as a request but stick firmly to your position.

K. Ultimatums - (also known as, take it or leave it)

If your negotiating style includes the use of ultimatums then consider changing your style. Ultimatums are often a counter productive technique that can work against your intentions. Threats and ultimatums cause Koreans to stiffen their resolve to win which causes them to hold their position more firmly.

If you are on the receiving end of an ultimatum remain calm. By their nature ultimatums generate emotion. Resist the temptation to strike back. Ultimatums can quickly escalate to confrontation and words may be exchanged that will be regretted later. At the first sign of an ultimatum take control of your emotions and work to calm the other side. Be careful not to say anything that would inflame their already excited state. With Koreans, show empathy, offer support, use tradeoffs or any other technique to assuage the NP's demands.

Continuing the discussion is always better than ending a relationship with a bad feeling. If you can compromise do so by requesting a concession from the other side. One method often used in place of negotiating changes to a written contract is to simply change the items you want, sign it and return it. If the changes are not too offensive the NP may simply concede them without further discussion.

Buying, "as is," is a kind of ultimatum. A demand to buy "as is" does not prevent you from making a different offer, although many negotiators act as if it does. Submit a counter offer, the NP might just take it. For example, a positive counter offer could be: I know this car is for sale as is but if you take the two new tires off the other car and put them on this one I would buy it.

When a person proposes a take it or leave it offer their purpose is to convince you it is the maximum or minimum they are prepared to accept. They portray this offer as the final compromise. Negotiators may be intimidated by such an offer and accept it without further discussion. As a rule, test the ultimatum and propose a counter offer. While an ultimatum may truly be the last compromise it does not preclude you from presenting another offer, especially if it allows the other person to save face. With Koreans it can be effective to ignore their offer and deliver yours with a sincere face. Koreans are not likely to use the take it or leave it approach unless they are angry or doubt your sincerity. Show your sincerity by ignoring their offer and making a counter offer. Avoid countering with ultimatums, and never say what you will not do; It closes your options. If for some reason a negotiator decides to use an ultimatum it should come at the very end of the negotiation, never in the beginning. Ultimatums need not be confrontational. You may use an implied ultimatum with a softer approach. As an alternative to a firm take it or leave it, use an implied ultimatum like, "I have done the best I can, this is as low as I can go."

Although I do not recommend blunt ultimatums they can be useful when turned into a positive statement. For example, instead of saying if you can't deliver the item by next week I will take my business elsewhere, try a more positive rephrasing such as, an agreed delivery date of next week would mean a lot toward deciding to do business with your company. If in the end you intentionally want to deliver a powerful ultimatum to an opponent, document the terms of the ultimatum to give it legitimacy. Negotiators consider the written word more seriously.

COUNTER TECHNIQUE

Don't accept ultimatums, let the ultimatum be the beginning of a new negotiation. As long as two sides are talking there is a chance of reaching an agreement. Ask for clarification of the ultimatum. Additional information can provide opportunities for counter offers.

Delay is a suitable defense in some cases. If an ultimatum is made in anger a delay can sometimes help soothe any bad feelings and allow time for you to pursue constructive and positive alternatives.

Put yourself on the same side as the NP. Look, I understand the reason for your offer but I think if we work together we can come up with some other solutions. If you are a seller, divert attention to a different product. The Itaewon salesman is well practiced at this. When you ask him to cut $20 off the price of a leather jacket he will quickly point to a cheaper jacket and try to convince you to buy it instead.

L. SPLIT THE DIFFERENCE

This is probably the most primitive of all the techniques and the one used most often, yet it is also the one most misunderstood. Most bargainers think that by splitting the difference they are being fair to both sides. But there is a method of success for even this simplest of techniques. The truth is the first person to split is usually the loser because there is almost always more than one split. For example, you are shopping in Namdaemun Market and spot an attractive sweater. You are told the price is $100 and you offer $60. After some haggling you suggest splitting the difference at $80. The saleslady sees you appreciate the fine garment and thanks you for your offer of $80. She then points out the quality of the material and the double stitching and agrees to split the difference between $80 and $100, - $90. By now you can see that had she been the first to split the difference you could have asked for the second split between $80 and $60, - $70 thus saving yourself $20 more. This is a simple example with small sums but unwary splitters unnecessarily concede much larger sums fairly frequently. Timing is important. Use this technique as a last resort and only when the difference is small, time is running out, or when you are very close to a deal and no further movement is foreseen. Make sure to only split once if you are the first, to split.

M. DECOY OR RED HERRING

Diverting attention away from the real issue, decoys are a common tactic used by Korean NP's. One presentation is to pretend to want an item the seller doesn't have and settle for the item you really wanted in the first place. For example, a customer enters a store with the intention of buying a chest of drawers, but instead the customer asks for a style of dresser the store doesn't sell. After some feigned disappointment the customer agrees to settle for the chest he really wanted in the first place. Since ostensibly, it is not what the customer wanted it is naturally more comfortable for the customer to ask for a discount or negotiate a lower price.

Another variation is to create a non-existent problem then demand a concession to solve it. The North Koreans are fond of this. The classic example was used at the Korean Armistice talks. Both sides were to choose neutral nation negotiators along with their own. The South chose three nations that were non-controversial and raised no objections. The North chose Poland, Czechoslovakia and the Soviet Union. No one could logically argue the Soviet Union was a neutral nation but the North Koreans insisted. They could have easily chosen another acceptable nation but they refused. When the talks stalemated, they offered to suggest a different country but demanded a concession in return. In fact, they were attempting to obtain a concession for a point that should not even have been in dispute. It was a masterful stroke and it worked to their advantage.

N. EMOTIONAL CLOSE

Sellers know that if a customer becomes emotionally attached to an item, the customer will often pay more or buy something he does not necessarily want or need. From the moment a customer has an item in hand, the emotional attachment begins. That's why 30-day free trials are so effective. It is why a car dealer may offer to let you take a car home over the weekend before you decide whether to buy. Thinking negotiators will try to introduce emotion if there is a chance it will be effective. For example, just think how happy you will be once you get this new stereo home. You have wanted this for a long time. Shall I go ahead and ring it up? The Emotional Close can be quite powerful, especially if you do not recognize it.

COUNTER TECHNIQUE

Remove the emotion and reintroduce objectivity. Review the facts of the deal and stay focused.

O. RELUCTANT BUYER/ SELLER

Imagine for a moment, a young lady walks into a store in Itaewon and spies that antique chest she always wanted. Her face lights up with joy. Turning to her friend she remarks, "This is it. My journey is over. It's just what I've always dreamed of. I just have to buy it." The store clerk who has been quietly watching approaches. "Can I help you" she asks with a big smile. "Yes, I was admiring this wonderful piece. It's beyond my wildest expectations and it seems to be in perfect condition. I've seen similar pieces in far worse condition sell for $1,000. I've lived in Korea for two years and wouldn't you know I would end my search just before we move back to America. If we hurry I just might arrange for it to be included in my household goods shipment back to the USA. What are you asking for it?"

How much easier could this person have made the sales clerk's job? How much information and negotiating power has the customer given away unnecessarily? The customer raved about the chest and told the sales clerk her deadline of purchasing in time for her household goods shipment. The sales clerk has a clear negotiating advantage. Do situations like this ever happen? Everyday! By reacting so honestly and extemporaneously shoppers forfeit their leverage before the negotiation begins. Always begin an inquiry as if you are not that interested but could be convinced to buy a product. If you are the seller, always act as if you don't really want to sell but would for the right price. Don't break this rule easily. You may even go so far as to hold out until the end and then ask bluntly "well I'm not sure I really want to buy/sell but what would you ask/offer." Of course, if the item you desire is a hot seller you may not want to act too reluctant as there are likely plenty of other customers eager to replace you. Every person has a price range whether buying or selling. Playing reluctant buyer/seller can help nudge the person closer to your figure before the negotiation even starts. If you envision an easy negotiation ahead you are less likely to move away from your ideal range. Koreans are natural reluctant buyers/sellers. They don't like to rush into deals, as they view patience as a virtue. Sometimes their silence alone is interpreted as reluctance. Don't fear their reluctance but deal with it by making them feel good about the negotiation.

COUNTER TECHNIQUE

Be reluctant also. Both sides can play this game effectively. A relevant seller can expose a reluctant buyer and vice verse.

P. PASS THE MONKEY

If possible, put the pressure on the NP by a simple, You'll have to better than that. When I told a retailer I was not happy with the price of a pool table he included delivery and some accessories free. I didn't need to say anything further. Koreans may say that your offer is not acceptable and remain silent. Once again, don't panic. Invite the NP to state what he feels is acceptable and begin, the negotiation. By transferring to the NP, the pressure to act, you better position yourself to ultimately gain the advantage.

COUNTER TECHNIQUE

Ask the NP to state what he wants. Pressure the NP to make the offer, don't volunteer an offer.

Q. NIBBLING

This technique is so common it has several names such as slicing and the last minute add on. When faced with a nibble, review the basics. The nibble is known well to Koreans, especially in agreements that are not written down or specifically spelled out. But it can be used effectively against Koreans as well. In it's simplest form the car sale provides the perfect example. While negotiating the purchase of a used car in Seoul, I effectively agreed on a price both sides could live with. Just before the papers were to be signed I mentioned, the deal does include new mud flaps and plastic air foils over the windows, doesn't it? The extra trim was popular at that time and normally list priced at about $200. The salesman, not wanting to lose the deal over a small add on relented and I felt happy with my purchase. Nibblers rarely ask for everything during the negotiation. They consciously save certain items until the end hoping to win a surprise deal clinching concession. If unprepared, the other side reaches the point where they already feel a deal is clinched and are emotionally prepared to end the negotiation. When the nibble is presented, they do not want to lose that precious deal so they concede. Of course, nibbling is a great way to politely work your way out of a deal you do not really want. Your Korean NP too, may nibble to discourage you and end a deal without hard feelings. Because it is sometimes difficult for Koreans to say no they may ask for more concessions than you are willing to give in order to create enough pressure to persuade you to back away from the deal yourself. In this way they can end the negotiation without creating an enemy.

COUNTER TECHNIQUE

Use conditional trade off, if I agree to do this will you agree to do that? In the above example, the car salesman could have countered with, "No that wasnt mentioned in our discussion but I am willing to offer you a good deal on the extras or well, I will include the trim if you allow us to install it at your expense." Conditional trade-off may be used as a counter to any demand for a concession. Some negotiators will agree to the nibble if it's a deal clincher — I'll do that if it clinches the deal. This introduces an end point and stops the nibbler from making more demands. Another effective counter technique is to identify it and ask the NP to stop. When presented at the last minute with a nibble you should say kindly to your Korean NP, we are very close to an end here, would you feel comfortable if I added a few more demands at this point in our discussions? If they really want the agreement they will back off. You may also use higher authority or good guy bad guy to stop nibbling. Last minute add-ons may not always be a nibble. An executive from a leading Korean construction corporation revealed to me a situation that occurred in the Middle East. The Korean company had negotiated a deal in the hundreds of millions of dollars. They spent nearly two years preparing the details and gaining government approvals. To close the deal they scheduled an elaborate signing ceremony that included high level corporate and Minister level government officials.

Shortly before the ceremony, a representative of the Middle East government informed the Korean negotiators that they required an additional $2 million more for the Minister or the deal would fall through. The Koreans were shocked and angered but they huddled and agreed to pay the extra fee rather than spoil the opportunity for the large contract and endure the embarrassment of a cancellation at such a moment. The technique proved very effective for the Minister. However, I am confident the cost was later incorporated into the contract in other ways.

COUNTER TECHNIQUE

When faced with an unpleasant add-on counter with a conditional trade off, "if I agree to do this will you agree to do that?"

R. DISCOVER DEFECTS

Finding blemishes in a product provides a reason to lower the price. I first discovered the value of this in a most unlikely place in America — K-mart. While searching for some wood chips to spread around the fence line of my home, I was disappointed with the quality of the product available. I noticed the bags had small tears in them and although the holes were not big enough to lose any of the contents I didn't feel comfortable buying them. I explained my concern to the sales person and offered to buy them at 1/2 price. Surprisingly he accepted. I have never paid full price for those type items since. Americans are acquainted with negotiating such discounts on blemished tires, lower grade apparel and other items. I recommend thoroughly searching for such defects when making any purchase. I have found Koreans use the technique extensively. They often point out defects and appear disappointed, never angry. When nego-

tiating with Koreans, politely point out the defects without criticizing and propose a reasonable offer as just compensation. Be
careful not to over criticize, just objectively identify defects.
Remember this rule, perceived defects are defects. For example,
that color red is just too dark, I wanted something lighter. While
there is nothing wrong with the color, it is a defect to you and
can be presented as a legitimate negotiating point.

COUNTER TECHNIQUE

Offer items "as is" to deflate the defect argument. When an
NP mentions a defect, direct his attention toward all the positive points on your side.

S. TEAM APPROACH

A negotiating team can be a powerful force in your favor if it is
assembled properly. A poor mixture can produce disaster.
Choosing whether to field a team or a single negotiator
depends on several factors such as expense and complexity of
the negotiation. Each approach has specific advantages. A team
can be effective when a negotiation is complex and special skills
are needed. When negotiating internationally, cost is often a factor. Dispatching a team overseas can be overly expensive. If you
decide to use a team approach take the time to gather the team
far in advance of negotiations and ensure all members agree
with the negotiation strategy. Assign roles and insist team members stay within their assignments. If you are traveling to Korea,
complete this preparation in the U.S., then review it again after
arrival in Korea. Having the wrong team members or members
with their own agenda can ruin a negotiation or provide the
opponent with unnecessary advantages.

When you meet the NP's team take time to know each one. The young member you meet today may be a senior negotiator the next time you meet. At times junior members of a Korean team may remain while senior members rotate. Having good rapport with all members is like an insurance policy. Be alert for internal conflict within the NP's team. Assign some of your team members to look for verbal and nonverbal signs of internal disagreement. Watch out for leaks, even unintentional, by loose-lipped members. The NP will be scouting your team for internal conflicts and for members susceptible to being co-opted. Thoroughly brief your members on the importance of discipline and enforce it throughout the negotiation. Experts agree there are a number of advantages to a team approach. One advantage is the specialized knowledge that can be part of the negotiation if you include individuals with technical or other specialized skills. The team approach has the added advantage of collective judgment. The observations of team members along with their advice can be a tremendous boost.

One problem with harmonious groups is group think. The group may become stubbornly reluctant to entertain new ideas and will actually resist their introduction. Frank and open discussion is not rewarded in those groups. Keep your team emotionally together but mentally independent. Members must feel comfortable introducing new ideas.

One advantage of a single negotiator is the NP cannot take advantage of the inexperienced or disloyal members of a group. So if you are employing a team it must be clear to all members that there is only one spokesman for the group. All comments and discussion within the group should be done in private.

If your team can infiltrate or co-opt the NP's team you can gain advantage. Try to draw one of their group to your side.

Observe their group and select at least one person who is either sympathetic or friendly and befriend him. Let that person be your unwitting advocate. You can also use this person as a conduit to leak information to the NP.

Remember, the NP may try to sow discord or create disagreement among your team members. Koreans will wine & dine your members to win their support. Monitor all team member contact closely.

Having a team has the added advantage of presenting the NP with the impression of a more formidable opposition. The number of members on your team should be discussed in advance and should be based on the overall situation including cost, need, and how many members the NP will use. Members should protect each other from unwittingly making decisions contrary to the overall strategy.

Teams may actually negotiate one level at a time, for example, a director negotiates first, then the managing director negotiates further and finally the Chairman negotiates and closes the deal. I used this technique effectively in negotiating a lease. The lowest ranking member of the team negotiates the general framework in accordance with pre-set guidelines. The next level negotiator refines the agreement leaving only the simplest issues for the Chairman, or other executive to finalize.

T. Power Negotiators

Power negotiating is a technique all it's own. It combines the methods of a few negotiating styles with the intent of intimidating to gain an advantage. The negotiator's edge is to dazzle an opponent with size, status or wealth. American power negotiators will typically insist on negotiating in their environs (bring opponents to their turf). They will try to impress opponents with a stylish office, secretary, staff and impressive photos of the power negotiator with important people. In fact, power negotiators often display an entire "I love me" wall full of plaques and awards. During the meeting they will take important telephone calls and often drop names of important people they know. In short, they will use every means to inflate their status and use this advantage to drive down their opponents offer or gain some other negotiating advantage. Americans have become sensitized to this type of negotiator and are not as easily impressed.

Koreans also power negotiate and will attempt to establish themselves in a higher social position than their opponent. The best advice is that if you decide to power negotiate in Korea, do it with dignity and courtesy. IMPRESS but don't INSULT. Demonstrate, through your good manners and demeanor, that you are a *gwibin* VIP. Apologize for interruptions but allow them. Be kind but firm and dignified. Most Koreans will be impressed and even envious of the status and more often than not rush to develop a relationship. The danger is if the technique is overdone the Korean NP will be insulted and flee from your presence never to return. Power negotiators look for the non verbal reaction and then follow up immediately. Some negotiators call this looking for the flinch. I knew a successful Korean publisher who sold advertisements that way. When selling advertisement space in his magazine to foreigners he advised quoting the advertisement price, and if the customer didn't flinch, adding 200,000 won for translation and if they still didn't flinch adding 200,000 won for production. Surprisingly often it actually worked.

COUNTER TECHNIQUE

Smart negotiators identify the Power Negotiating tactic and ask for another meeting at a time and place more suitable and free from interruptions. Ironically, this tactic can work well with Koreans who respect status and power. You can counter American Power Negotiators by slightly embarrassing them. If an American is showing off by accepting several phone calls during your discussion tell him you would rather schedule another meeting when he is not so busy.

If an NP is dropping names to impress you, it is perfectly acceptable to play the same game by dropping a few names of your own and then suggesting a more pertinent discussion of the specific issues. For example, an encounter might transpire like this.

Mr. Jones: Hi Mr. Kim, nice to meet you!

Mr. Kim: Hi Mr. Jones, nice to meet you also. I know your boss, Mr. White very well. I had lunch last week with White and his boss Mr. Rudy. Nice fellows.

Mr. Jones: Oh great, I know your Managing Director Mr. Lee, very well, and I was invited to a party at the Chairman's home last month. We had a great discussion on cooperation concerning these manufacturing specifications I have brought with me. Let me show you.

Matching an opponent's name-dropping can nullify the technique. However, it must be performed with tact. With Korean Power negotiators, another strategy is to play along without causing them to lose face, but do not appear overly impressed. Always be polite regardless of status and regardless of how annoying their personalities may be.

U. MITIGATE THE DIFFERENCE

Portray the distance between the two final positions as insignificant in order to convince the NP to move his position in your direction. This technique is best used against emotional negotiators or Koreans trying to save face. Give the impression to the NP that the deal is near closing and it would be improper for a man of his status to haggle over insignificant differences. Example, An important man like you wouldn't argue over $1,000 would you?

V. CONDITIONAL OFFER

An offer with a hidden condition. For example, I am willing to pay the stated price only if you will agree to a penalty for late delivery. Another example, I will pay the asking price for this office if you throw in the small office next door to accommodate my future expansion. Conditional offers are effective when proposed as deal clinchers timed to seal a negotiation.

W. BLUFF

If presented properly, a bluff can be a powerful tool of persuasion. I had a colleague who was a master of the bluff at hotels. He would approach the desk and ask for a room. The clerk would quote a price, for example $100. The man would insist he had stayed at the hotel two months ago and the price was only $65 per night. He would say, Check your records. The hotel clerk couldn't or wouldn't check the records so he conceded the discount. I have seen him use this and similar bluffs scores of times. The key is to be sincere when you deliver it, you must believe it yourself.

X. TAKE IT BACK

What do you do when you think a negotiation is concluded and at the next meeting the proposals are withdrawn in some way? This can be truly embarrassing but it does happen and Koreans are not afraid to use this tactic if need be. I remember negotiating legal fees with a firm already servicing our company and coming to a verbal agreement. A short time later, the home office refused to accept the price. I had to return to the Law Firm and offer a lesser amount for services already rendered (a very embarrassing situation). Obviously, the Law Firm was not happy. They launched personal attacks, guilt, threats, and everything else to convince our company to honor the verbal agreement. After remaining unemotional and firm to our position, the negotiations started again. We were eventually able to reach an agreement satisfactory to both sides.

COUNTER TECHNIQUE

Identify any higher authority before the end of negotiation and ensure the NP has full authority to negotiate terms. If a proposal is taken back then it is your right to reopen the negotiation on all points, not just the point NP has emphasized. If the proposal was rejected by a higher authority, demand identification of the higher authority and consider negotiating directly with them.

CHAPTER 6

Successfully Negotiating with Koreans

Successfully Negotiating with Koreans

A. VIEW THINGS FROM THEIR ANGLE

> *Even a sheet of paper becomes lighter when it is carried*
> *by two persons.*
> "종이 한 장도 맞들면 낫다."
> — Korean Proverb

> *Secret of success, being able to see things from*
> *anothers point of view.*
> — Henry Ford

Koreans appreciate those who can see their side of an argument. Americans often press their point without trying to understand the opponent's point of view. Perceptions are critical. Even if you absolutely understand an opponents viewpoint make sure the NP clearly acknowledges your sensitivity to his side of the argument. Cultural differences can cause terrible misunderstanding. Just imagine the following examples of two different points of view that could cause misunderstanding and impede a successful negotiation.

Korean	American
I am a good employee, I always do what I'm told.	You are a poor performer, I always have to tell you to do something before you do it.
I have a terrible boss. My personal life is private and I hate probing questions.	I am a good boss. I am concerned with my employees so I always ask about their personal lives.

Well intentioned people send unintended messages due to unrecognized cultural differences. Don't let yourself unwittingly fall into this troublesome trap.

Convince the NP that you understand him completely before you present your position. Before you can put yourself on the same side as the NP you must diffuse any suspicion of competition between you. By not arguing with the NP you can diffuse competitiveness early in the negotiation. Avoid disagreement, concentrate on agreement. Be slow to reject the NP's ideas, show interest, try to understand his side. Concentrate on resolving problems, not placing blame.

Koreans respect a partner who can change with changing circumstances, Americans respect a partner who is reliable and keeps his word on contracts despite circumstances that have changed to his disadvantage. This is a potential cultural trap that quickly raises mistrust among NP's. If a situation changes after an agreement has been reached, Koreans will expect flexibility in a partner's actions. At the same time, the American side will regard the situation as a test of faithfulness and reliability. For example, a contract was negotiated for supplies to be delivered on May 15th. In February the company experiences an unexpected 30 day strike. The company tells the American customer of a projected delay due to the strike. If the American side demands strict adherence to the contract date even though the company loses money the Korean side will lose trust in the American side. If there ever is a future negotiation, the Korean NP will be looking for revenge or a way to undermine and sabotage the process. Conversely, in the above situation if the American side informs the Korean company that despite the severe hardship the delay is causing, the American side will work for a compromise delivery date in the hopes of cementing the relationship and securing future business together and reap the benefits of cooperation at the next negotiation. In Korea, resorting to litigation is often an indicator of failure.

B. CREATE A FAVORABLE NEGOTIATION SURROUNDINGS

> *When you know the opponents as well as yourself,*
> *you'll surely win every war against them.*
> "知彼知己(지피지기)면 百戰百勝(백전백승)"
> — Korean Proverb

The significance of space is not a new concept. Even King Arthur made a round table to symbolize equal status among the knights. Personal and physical space arrangements are important to Koreans. Where a person (especially leaders) sits and the order of seating around a table has significance. Koreans feel comfortable arranging seating according to rank, status or seniority. Americans often pay little attention to such matters. When negotiating with Koreans rethink how you approach even basic elements such as seating. Be sensitive to seniority and status among members.

The environment tells your Korean NP a lot about you. Ask yourself, what does my office, car or other place say about me? Is my space dirty and dull, or is it professional, and does it project importance? Koreans will form an impression from this visual information, so help them to form a positive one.

Don't allow the environment to be a distraction. I remember meeting with an NP at a top hotel in Seoul, an informal negotiation. My interpreter was completely distracted by the fine buffet provided. He kept eyeing the buffet instead focusing on his work. I had to move the meeting to a spot totally away from the food to allow him to focus.

We have all seen pictures of diplomats and labor leaders negotiating across a table from each other. Tables are useful tools but at times they may create an unwanted barrier. A high table or desk can create uneasiness or undesired formality while a low coffee table can help relax the parties involved. On occasion, a barrier is desired but at other times it is an unwelcome obstacle. Dispense with a table if an informal format is more comfortable. In fact, switch the entire site to someplace more casual. Golf courses, restaurants, and room salons are often ideal places to negotiate. In Korea, the actual deal is often clinched outside the office. Gage your NP and determine if the situation merits changing the location to a more informal environment.

As previously mentioned, location is an important component of negotiation. Most negotiators acknowledge that negotiating on home turf affords a distinct advantage. It generates confidence in you and causes the opponent to feel uneasy because he is negotiating on unfamiliar ground. However, protocol in Korea demands that if meeting with a person of higher status you should visit their location. Experts argue that by visiting the NP's location you demonstrate sincerity and respect for local custom. The symbolism can work to your advantage. It may also produce the opposite effect. By coming to Korea to negotiate you may have unknowingly robbed an executive of a chance for the foreign travel he was looking forward to. However, if you concede location because of the NP's status then negotiate some advantage in return. For example, if the NP insists on negotiating in Korea then ask that the actual meeting be held in a neutral site, like the conference room of a major hotel. Choose a site not frequented by the NP and arrive a few days early to familiarize yourself with the territory. If the NP is power negotiating and insists on meeting in his office, you can still try to disorient him by moving from behind a desk to the side or insisting you all sit in the sofa area. In the end, exercise all possible options and never totally accede to his demands.

If you must visit Korea to negotiate use your time wisely to gather as much information about the NP as possible. Visit his business, visit competitors, talk with the American Chamber of Commerce, the US Embassy, or other Chambers of Commerce, about the NP. You will obtain valuable tips from each source. For example, the US Embassy may yield certain bits of knowledge concerning the NP while the British Chamber of Commerce may know the NP more intimately and serve as a wealth of information. Broaden your net of information gathering.

Environment can be used by the seller to deflect attention to a lower priced item during negotiation. If you are negotiating on the NP's home turf it may be convenient for him to introduce items or issues for which you were not prepared. For example, you are negotiating the purchase of a piece of property in Busan, with a Korean company, and you are standing firm on a specific price. The NP suggests you consider purchasing a different, less expensive, site and offers to take you to see it. Since you are in Busan the pressure would be great for you to at least visit the property. However, if you were not negotiating this stage on his turf, (in Busan) the opportunity to distract you would not present itself. It would be to your benefit to negotiate that specific portion of the agreement in Seoul, or by phone.

Koreans practice naturally what the experts teach about luring officials out of the official environment to achieve success.

Koreans are quick to invite you away from the safety of your own environment to the comfort of theirs. There is nothing wrong with this approach, as a matter of fact it is recommendable. But if you are the invitee you must be on guard so as not to be taken advantage of. While in Korea, make every effort to invite your NP out of his environment, not only for a negotiating advantage, but also as a basis for building a solid relationship.

Americans feel comfortable with informal relationships, Koreans with more formal relationships. However, there is a place for informality and Koreans love to go there to develop friendships. Drinking establishments are the places where Koreans remove their formal faces and allow their informal faces to emerge. A visit usually involves a night of singing, dancing and much revelry. It is an unwritten code however, that the goings on inside those establishments remains private and should be shared only with those who were present. Outside these places, it is wise to keep a certain formality in your public interactions. We will talk about a more exact meaning of formality in another chapter.

C. SELL YOURSELF FIRST

Every long journey starts with a step.
"천 리 길도 한 걸음부터"

Whether you are in government, business, sales, a tourist or in any other negotiating scenario you must concentrate on selling yourself and building a relationship with the negotiating partner. If the person you are negotiating with can believe you, if he can trust you, your chance of success increases dramatically. The depth and effort involved in selling yourself varies depending on the situation. If you are a salesman, who negotiates with the same buyer frequently, selling yourself may be a constant and expensive effort. If you are a shopper in a Korean market, who may never see the merchant again, you would still be wise to spend time talking with that person and establishing rapport for a short period before entering into negotiation. Selling yourself should start with the first meeting and never stop. Start well. Begin with an impressive entrance. Always enter a room smiling and be attentive to the NP. Utilize a favorable first impression to build a strong relationship. Selling yourself is the foundation of relationship building, the focus of the next section.

State the purpose of negotiation specifically, with clearly defined points. Project professionalism and establish your credibility. It is vital that the NP respects you. If the first negotiation is successful, subsequent negotiations usually proceed smoothly based on the trust built between parties. Foreigners who neglect firmly strengthening their credibility, from the initial phase of contact, are grading a steeper path to future success. If you can create a few small negotiating successes early, bigger successes will follow. While everyone strives to negotiate the "Big Deal" it is more difficult and the chance of failure is great. It may be to your advantage to negotiate a smaller matter with a high chance of success as a building block to further negotiations.

When presenting your position, relate your justification and rationale to your experiences or better yet, the NP's experiences. When possible, offer analogies to Korean history. It will not only increase the NP's willingness to understand your position, the

NP will appreciate your knowledge of Korea and you will gain favor in his eyes. Analogies need not be sophisticated. Simple mention of a historical event or character can illustrate the point. I remember a savvy foreigner trying to explain to a small group of Koreans the importance of a few key members in the American company they were dealing with. He was trying to explain that Mr. Jones was a wise old, scholarly member, highly respected in the company and the entire industry. The foreigner jokingly proclaimed him the King Sejong of the company. While the analogy itself was poor, his Korean audience enjoyed it. They were surprised the American even knew of King Sejong and the unexpected mention of him made the group relax and feel more comfortable with the American.

Negotiating continues into social events. Remember, you are making an impression that will influence their decisions far beyond the logic of your arguments. One of the purposes of the social events is to encourage all parties to loosen up. Be careful not to let your guard down too far however, as your Korean NP will be watching you closely. Join in the fun and enjoy but maintain your dignity. Koreans are well known as great hosts and their hospitality can sometimes pressure Americans to reciprocate the kindness by making concessions in negotiations.

Dress well. Koreans dress for all occasions. Look sharp and avoid casual wear for all business functions. Americans tend to view casual dress as more appropriate for developing a friendly relationship but Korean businessmen are likely to meet in more formal business attire.

Protect your good name, it is critical in Korea. Kim Woo-choong the founder of Daewoo Corporation and one of

---

[1] Kim Woo-choong, *Every Street is Paved with Gold* (Singapore: Times Books International, 1992), p. 79.

Korea's leading businessmen advised that whatever you do always protect your name and your integrity. If losing your life is personal death then losing your reputation is social death, he said.[1] Korea is a small country and word travels fast so guard your reputation jealously. A respectable reputation is worth points in most negotiations because an agreement is most often based on trust. If trust exists, the struggle is half won. If trust is weak you are likely headed for disaster. Determine which aspect of your company's reputation can be used to your advantage. For example, I worked for a Korean company that had the reputation of completing projects quickly. As far as I was concerned the reputation was undeserved but we often used it to our advantage in international negotiation. While working in a third world country I discovered the locals assumed our company was hard working just because we were a Korean company. Korean companies had the reputation of being hardworking and we used that to our advantage in negotiating.

D. BUILD POSITIVE RELATIONSHIPS

> As for clothes, the newer the better,
> as for friends the older, the better.
> "옷은 새것이 좋고 친구는 오래될수록 좋다."
> — Korean Proverb

> Am I not destroying my enemies when I make friends of them?
> — Abraham Lincoln

> The only way to have a friend is to be one.
> — Ralph Waldo Emerson

For Koreans, the process of reaching an agreement is as important as the result. The relationship between all parties must be harmonious and pleasant. Koreans want to ensure that when the inevitable hard times occur, their partner will be flexible and easy to work with, not rigid and legalistic.

Koreans expect friends to be understanding even if they disagree, so sympathize with your friend when he's relating his problems. This is no time to be objective. Koreans want empathy not objectivity from friends. Treat the NP similarly. If the Korean NP raises a valid point agree and acknowledge it. He will appreciate it and such good manners will help strengthen the relationship. Of course moderation is always sound advice. Be agreeable without being a sycophant.

Koreans favor a sense of confidentiality. Keep the deal or details of the agreement secret. Even an Itaewon merchant may confide, I'll give you a good price but don't tell anyone. He is trying to create an impression that the customer is receiving a special bargain. In all forms of negotiations, it's wise to convince the NP he is receiving special treatment. Convince the Korean NP he is obtaining exclusivity, obtaining it the easy way, the way no one else can. For Example, I worked for a Korean executive that made his Korean NP believe he was able to receive special deals because of his personal relationship with the Chairman of the large corporation. Whether he actually had such a relationship was never demonstrated but the NP believed it and agreed to work together.

Quiet acts of deference may solidify a relationship. I recall a retired executive who worked as a special consultant for an NP's company. In his previous position he was a senior executive in a large corporation. Since coming out of retirement he accepted a somewhat lower advisory position in the new company. During negotiations we took great pains to treat the gentleman with the respect he was used to in his previous position. He appreciated this immensely. In return he gave us the benefit of the doubt on several important matters that helped our side tremendously in our negotiation.

Symbolism and ritual are meaningful in relationships. Learn the symbols and rituals respected by your NP and incorporate them, where possible, into your routine. Symbols and rituals include everything from a Saturday morning golf match, to after work saunas or evening drinks. Partake in these rituals if invited. Participating in business rituals will expose you to the more private world of Korea. Koreans are more candid in private, but endeavor to keep their official face in public. By entering the private world you may obtain an advantage in negotiation.

Koreans view contracts differently than you may suppose. For Americans the contract is king and must be adhered to religiously. For Koreans, a contract can mean little more than the initial test of the relationship. In a sense, it is merely a symbol of a commitment to work together. They will expect you to be receptive to proposed changes after the contract is signed. Friends are expected to empathize and help each other. Obviously, international Korean companies tend to follow Western business practices more closely. However, it is common for foreigners who either remain ignorant of or ignore Korean business customs to experience severe difficulty at some point. Even between Koreans disagreements arise. In October 1998, Hyundai founder Jeong Ju-Yeong, negotiated a ground breaking deal with North Korea to allow cruise ships to call at Jangjeon Port and the tourists to visit the scenic Mt. Geumgang. This $940 million deal was well on it's way. Tourists had actually begun to visit when contract difficulty appeared. Hyundai apparently negotiated for rights to the project for a long time, obviously vague language designed to sidestep disagreement and begin the project quickly. Hyundai later specified they desired the negotiated terms for 30 years, but the North Koreans quickly balked, even though they had agreed to grant Hyundai the rights to Jangjeon port for 50 years. This unnecessary miscalculation caused a delay in the project. [2]

Strong relationship building will earn you the close calls. As an American, you may think you are negotiating a contract but in the Orient you are negotiating a relationship. Koreans will give the benefit of the doubt to the party they are closer with regardless of the logic of the deal. In other words, all else being equal, the party with the better relationship wins.

E. MAINTAIN A POSITIVE ATTITUDE / AVOID CONFRONTATION

Nobody can spit on a smile.
"웃는 얼굴에 침 못 뱉는다"
— Korean Proverb

Agree with thine adversary quickly.
— Matthew 5:25

The gentleman agrees with others without being an echo, the small man echoes without being in agreement.
— Confucius

All conflict need not be resolved - some can be avoided.
— Herb Cohen

---

[2] Korea Herald, "North Lashes out at South, U.S. for trying to use mountain tour for political purposes." 12-31-98. www.Koreaherald.co.kr

People love to agree. Few are good losers. It is wise not to create enemies. By losing your cool you may not only jeopardize one deal you may damage future negotiations. Korea is a small country and your reputation (both positive and negative) will spread quickly. Koreans often attend initial meetings with a formal face. As a foreigner, greet them with a smile. A cheerful expression can soften their mood and begin the meeting on a positive note. Maintain a pleasant attitude throughout the contacts, even when situations become ugly.

Slipping into a confrontation with your Korean NP can be extremely difficult to recover from. Confrontations destroy harmony and the willingness of the other side to continue discussion. When a long-standing adversarial relationship exists, for example, US-North Korea, management-labor, or feuding neighbors, negotiations are obviously more strained. Past problems are seldom forgotten and will certainly become part of the equation in any ongoing negotiation. The fundamental approach is to attempt to establish a relationship both in and out of the negotiation. Search for common ground, initiate dialog and most of all, LISTEN. Define problems in a way that both sides may agree. Use these methods to at least plant the seeds of trust and empathy. Even though your proposal has weaknesses you should never apologize, present it with the confidence that it is the best, without boasting.

Good manners are imperative. Koreans react positively to proper manners. Once just before a flight, I was trying to upgrade an employees airline ticket using frequent flyer miles but the person was 500 miles short of a legitimate upgrade. The ticket agent was extremely busy and having a difficult time with a number of impatient, angry customers. She refused my request and braced for an emotional tirade. Instead, I calmly and politely explained how important it was to me and asked if she could help. She smiled, relaxed and then agreed to post the miles for the flight before that flight was completed, and use those miles to upgrade the ticket. This solution was a serious bending of the rules but was performed because of the positive interaction we had.

Choice of words can mean all the difference in your success. Examine your expressions and consider rephrasing for positive effect. For example, a negative statement such as if you don't give me a discount I will find someone else to buy from, could be changed to you know, Im in a difficult situation at this point and lower prices would go a long way in helping us work out a solution beneficial to both of us. A simple change of words and tone of voice can mean the difference between acceptance and rejection. Koreans will respond much more favorable to a person who presents himself as a gentleman or *Yangban*.[3] Choose words and actions that will earn you the reputation of a *Yangban*.

Avoid criticism. I knew an American missionary who claimed to love Korea and Koreans. He lived there quite a few years. However, he had an annoying habit of criticizing Korean driving, in public settings, even during his sermons. He often complained about how crazy Koreans were when they got behind the wheel of a car and how rude Koreans could be while driving. It was always a tense and ugly moment when he spoke this way it detracted from his otherwise bright and cheerful sermons. I don't think he realized the harm he was doing because he was so impassioned about his view. Don't criticize publicly. At the very least it is rude. It forms a terrible impression that is difficult to overcome. Be reluctant to criticize privately, even if

---

[3] *Yangban* were gentleman scholars of Yi Dynasty Korea (1392-1910)

pressed soften your negative views severely.

Deal with negative people by countering them with a positive attitude. When I was younger I worked for a man some described as an egomaniac. The slightest show of initiative would send him into a tirade of how he was the boss and made the decisions, and how he didn't have to listen to subordinates. A few subordinates enjoyed pushing his hot button from time to time but when we really needed his approval we would disarm him with this approach, "I know you have thought of this already but might we not do better by implementing this idea......" or from our previous discussions I tried to put your ideas on paper what do you think? Even if we never had a previous discussion the person would agree as long as it appeared to be his idea. Hopefully you will never reach this extreme but the example does illustrate the importance of keeping matters positive.

Koreans are similar to Americans in that they demand acknowledgment that they were wronged. If you offend the NP apologize sincerely. If the NP raises a valid point, acknowledge it with a smile. It will help to build goodwill between both sides. Sometimes people just want to be right. Try not to fall into this trap yourself but if the NP needs to be told he is right develop it into a trade-off point. Acknowledge that he is right and then while he is in a good mood ask for a small concession in another area. Chances are he will agree.

F. Avoid Negative Emotion

Even a word only sometimes can pay a big debt.
"말 한마디로 천냥 빚을 갚는다"
— Korean Proverb

*When dealing with people, remember you are not dealing with
creatures of logic but creatures of emotion.*

— Dale Carnegie

Negative emotion is your enemy, it prevents you from thinking
straight. Thinking is the strength of a good negotiator. It is difficult to reason with an angry NP. When Koreans lose their temper, if you remain calm, and agree with them, they will slowly
calm themselves. Afterwards, they may feel shame and allow
concessions to save face. Stimulate positive feelings in the NP
by suggesting terms and items that will benefit him. Negative
feelings last a long time. It is a Western notion that feelings
should have no part in a negotiation, that the entire negotiation
should be objective. In Korea it is quite different. Harmony, satisfaction, acceptance, and agreement are all intertwined into the
final outcome.

Don't pressure Koreans — they detest it and will stiffen
resistance. If you lose your cool, take a break, apologize and
begin again. It has been said that while people only remember
10% of what you say they clearly remember the entire emotional impact you make on them. Create a favorable impression and
it will continue pay dividends long after your words have been
forgotten.

One famous author and negotiator advised to differentiate
between gut decisions and gut reactions. Gut decisions are calculated and formed slowly after hearing all the facts. Gut reactions are made in the heat of the moment after hearing one fact.
With Koreans, it is OK to make gut decisions but steer away
from gut reactions. It is to your advantage to determine the
NP's hot buttons and avoid them.

As a tactic, fear does not work well with Koreans. In most

cases it backfires. Koreans possess a great pride and ability to endure severe hardship. If you insult or try to intimidate them they will resist to the very end. But pointing out dire consequences is a legitimate negotiating tool if performed properly. It is safe to explain that certain actions will result in unpleasant consequences if you are careful not to communicate it as a threat.

Never negotiate out of fear but never fear to negotiate.
— John F. Kennedy

A raised voice is a sign of lost self control. Maintain your composure in all circumstances. It is a sign of good manners and will signal that you are a person worthy of doing business with. Americans sometimes feel that letting off steam in a meeting demonstrates their power. Americans may use a display of power for effect. Unfortunately such displays of emotion will normally produce the wrong effect in Korea!

G. Develop a Patience / Persistence Long term Perspective

The repreated stroke will fell the oak.
"열번 찍어 안넘어가는 나무 없다"
— Korean Proverb

He that can have patience can have what he will.
— Benjamin Franklin

Our patience will achieve more than our force.
— Edmund Burke

Recite "patience" three times and it will spare you a murder.
— Korean Proverb

Americans love to jump right into business, it's part of our culture. Most negotiators however, will advise against it even when negotiating among Americans. It is really an almost universal axiom. Koreans dislike delving directly into business matters. Be patient. Find something in common to talk about. A little preparation can help in this regard. A skilled negotiator gathers intelligence about the NP's likes and dislikes before a meeting. This information is used to facilitate casual conversation. Even if you are without such information it is not difficult to uncover a few items during regular conversation. Start by commenting on the NP's office, the view, the beauty of Seoul, or the wonders of Korea. Let the conversation develop from there. Keep the comments positive. During the conversation, shift to business slowly with a smooth transition.

Persist in the face of rejection. Rejection may not be as it appears. Koreans will often reject proposals on the first examination. They may not want to appear over eager, but do not be discouraged by their reluctance. Either try a different approach or rephrase your proposal and try again. Be persistent, but tactful.

Even though you have presented a persuasive argument, allow the Korean NP time to build consensus before giving you an answer, if needed. Patience is not just waiting, it can mean not pushing too hard. Silence is part of negotiation.

The more you talk the greater your chance of a slip of the tongue.
— Korean Proverb

You may experience silence or stalling if you ask the NP to exceed his authority. It may not be readily apparent because, it may be difficult for the NP to admit so without losing face, so be alert for signs that the NP is uncomfortable. Help him out of this predicament by offering alternatives that will solve his problem.

Silence for Koreans is more likely to indicate thinking not withdrawal or disinterest. Americans often fear silence as an indicator that something is going wrong in the discussion. Allow the NP an opportunity to think without being rushed. In most instances, the NP may not only have to prepare a response he may have the double responsibility of presenting it in a foreign language. This is no simple task and often requires careful thought. Afford the NP time to prepare his response without pressure. Don't talk for him. When a Korean NP is struggling to find the right words resist the temptation to interrupt with what you think he means. It can be frustrating and embarrassing for the NP. Allow the time needed to formulate a proper response. You can always clarify it after the fact.

Much of our behavior is predictable and so is our negotiating behavior. Observe the NP in a variety of situations, if possible, to learn of his reactions and techniques. Continue to observe him throughout the negotiation process. Document verbal and nonverbal indicators or patterns of behavior. Use your observations to your negotiating advantage.

H. Don't Reveal Weaknesses

Cautions about gossiping others.
"낮말은 새가 듣고 밤말은 쥐가 듣는다"
— Korean Proverb

Americans sometimes mention their personal or situational problems as a sign of openness or trust. Be careful not to reveal such items either intentionally or unintentionally. Personal weaknesses should be kept to yourself. It is quite amazing what negative information people freely reveal about themselves. Be careful that your behavior does not inadvertently reveal a weakness to your opponent.

Be reluctant to discuss the shortcomings of others. An executive I knew had an unfortunate habit of gossiping about others. This was annoying to a Korean executive he was trying to do business with. The Korean executive was obviously uncomfortable with such topics. The two never worked well together and I believe that was one of the major reasons. Korea is a land of intricate networks and it is difficult to tell who may be connected to whom. Gossip is unbecoming and will leave a bad impression.

Deadlines should be considered confidential, as they will certainly be used against you. If, for whatever reason, you must conclude an agreement by a specific date, your NP will likely stall negotiations until the minute hoping to win concessions. If you are able to impose a deadline on your opponent however, it can work to your advantage.

I. THIRD PARTY

Arms will bend inside only.
"팔이 안으로 굽는다"
— *Korean Proverb*

A third party can be decisive in resolving problems in a negotiation. In fact, negotiators should consider a third party for assistance before there is a problem. Third parties are helpful in keeping relations amicable. Are you faced with a tough NP that you would rather not negotiate with? A sympathetic third party can arrange for his replacement with someone more agreeable. A third party can help insure you negotiate at the appropriate level and may even be able to arrange the proper introductions. Knowing who to negotiate with can be as important as knowing how to negotiate. Dealing with a large Korean company or bureaucracy can be confusing. Selecting the proper person to contact should not be left to chance. Finding a specific contact friendly to you could assure success. A third party can suggest the appropriate level and even the proper person to deal with. These are just two of the many, small but effective uses of a third party in Korean negotiations. Identifying the correct third party is worth the effort. If by chance there is a third party sympathetic to your position, use him. During the Preparation Stage instruct your team members to identify possible third party candidates both sides know and respect. Remember, a third party has to be acceptable to both parties, a person both sides trust. If approached by an NP with a suggestion of a third party, do your homework. Try to determine your common interests. Look for places you have both visited, organizations you both belong to, common friends, etc. Don't assume because the NP Korean he has little in common with you. I remember a senior officer who could not develop a friendship with his Korean counterpart. He was being snubbed at every turn until he discovered they both were graduates of the University of Southern California. He used that and the assistance of another alumni to help them develop a relationship.

Third parties may include international organizations, religious organizations, a special interest group or an individual citizen. Third parties are helpful in proposing options you would like to propose but cannot in order to save face. A third party can propose a face saving compromise and break seemingly insurmountable deadlocks. Even between governments a third party can make the difference. In 1994, negotiations between North Korea and the U.S. were deadlocked. The U.S. was convinced that North Korea was not in compliance with agreed upon nuclear safeguards and was refusing to allow international inspections. North Korea charged the U.S. with interfering with it's internal affairs. Both countries were releasing hostile statements against each other and there was serious talk of possible war. Within this context former President Jimmy Carter traveled to North Korea to conduct discussions with Kim Il-sung. Acting as a third party, Carter was able to negotiate a compromise that temporarily averted war.

J. TRANSLATORS

What language should you speak in negotiation, English, Korean, both? This question is frequently debated and there are times when either language may be most appropriate. You place yourself at a disadvantage if you agree to use anything other than English but it is wise to consider providing Korean translation as a gesture. English may be the language of international conferences and high level business negotiations but having a translator could be helpful in various types of negotiations. Most Koreans employed in the international careers speak English but depending on the particular NP, a translator may permit the NP to feel more comfortable and allow him to relax. Not all NP's appreciate this luxury and some may actually be offended by it, if for example, the NP is fluent in English. Since there are times however, when a Korean translator could be appropriate, determine the feelings of the NP and analyze your specific rationale for wanting a translator.

If you use a translator, ensure the person knows the jargon of the NP in Korean. Assume the Korean translator is not familiar with specific industry jargon just as you would assume an American translator is unfamiliar with specific Korean jargon. Industry jargon can be a language of it's own. Individual trades require specific study to become proficient in their terminology. Direct the translator to study terminology and acronyms in both languages and test your translator before beginning a negotiation.

Strictly prohibit the translator from conversing independently with the NP without including you. I have seen translators conduct mini discussions with an NP then provide a short summary in English. A translator should never allow more than two or three sentences pass without translating back to you. The translator must work for you and defer to you. Carefully train your translator to keep you informed and not to take license with your words. This is a common problem with translators of all experience levels. Rather than admit they cannot translate what you said precisely, translations decide to try and convey your meaning in their own words. The meaning they convey can be considerably different than the intended one and can cause great confusion.

To rely on the NP's translator is to put yourself at risk. I have seen executives choose not to bring a translator because the NP will provide one. Remember that the translator will be loyal to NP and not you. This can be aggressively used to the NP's advantage.

Resolve to schedule a pre-meeting with your translator to

review phraseology, intent and terminology you expect to use in the negotiation. Always hold a debriefing, after a negotiating session to review what was said, what mistakes were made and how to improve in the next session. Program regular rest periods during the negotiation to keep your translator fresh. It is quite difficult and physically taxing to translate complex negotiations. Be kind to your translator and show due respect commensurate with age, education and position, however never allow the translator to upstage the negotiator.

Speak slowly, distinctly, and avoid slang. Do not use *banmal* or impolite language to your translator. Treat the person as a professional and with respect. Translators may be viewed as a real asset by Koreans, but they can also be subject to great pressure. Your NP may try to compromise your translator or convince him to switch loyalties. Always be on guard for indicators of such activity and test the translator frequently.

You should not hire someone to read or speak for your company just because they can read or write English. You should search for someone that has attained a certain level of proficiency which you decide is needed. Is the translator required to speak at a college level, graduate level? Don't assume every Korean speaks his language at a college level. Koreans are quick to acknowledge they are college graduates but what they mean is they have graduated with a two-year degree. If the translator has not attended college or even graduated from a two-year college, he may be incapable of dealing with higher level counterparts at their level. In addition, the translator may never earn the respect of the NP. In fact, the NP could even intimidate him. You may desire a translator with specialized experience in marketing, sales, or other technical field. Choose your translator carefully as it is a wise and useful investment.

K. THE LANGUAGE FACTOR

Americans often mistakenly believe that everyone in authority in a foreign country speaks English and if they don't, interpreters can easily fill the void. Those who take that position put themselves at a distinct disadvantage. Akio Morita, Chairmen of the Sony Corporation, reportedly was asked what was the most important language for an international businessman to know, "The language of the customer" was his reply. A wise answer but it is common for international businessmen to work in multiple countries and next to impossible for them to keep up with all of the languages they encounter. However, you are in Korea and it pays to learn at least some Korean. Even if you don't use it to negotiate a minimal proficiency in Korean is useful in social situations, which prepare the proper atmosphere for negotiating. Remember that a few words of Korean go a long way in building friendship and cooperation. Koreans notice and appreciate the foreigner who takes time to learn a little of their language. By becoming proficient basic greetings and polite expressions your Korean counterparts will be much more willing to work with you instead of against you.

In general, Koreans respond favorably to foreigners who speak their language. I remember traveling from Korea to another country on business. I had a ticket but forgot to confirm a reservation. Desperate to travel on that particular flight, I called the Asiana Airline counter and explained my situation. They apologized but said the flight was full. Still determined I went to the airport. The ticket agents were extremely busy and tersely gave me the same answer as I had received on the telephone — no space. I began to plead my case in the best Korean I could muster. As I spoke the representative's scowl turned into a smile. He asked me to wait while he would see what he could do. In a few minutes, he returned with my boarding pass. We chatted for a few minutes and he appreciated my attempt to speak in Korean. His English was excellent and my meager Korean broke no communication barriers. I'm sure however, it transformed me from just another customer with a problem into a person he wanted to help. He didn't say that's what made the difference but I'm convinced it played a major role. It is just one of thousands of personal examples where knowing even a little Korean has turned an ugly negotiating situation into a successful one.

Language differences can cause expensive mistakes. When a Korean company won a US government contract to replace miles of railroad track, the contract simply stated, replace old rails with new ones. After completion, it was discovered the Korean company replaced the old rails with old refurbished rails they had bought at a discount. While the contracting officer intended new to mean unused the Koreans successfully argued that new meant different. Just a little more specific language could have prevented the entire misunderstanding and subsequent legal battle. Once I asked a subordinate, who spoke both English and Korean fluently, to explain to another colleague a matter better expressed in his native tongue. The subordinate told the colleague that I wanted her to explain it in Korean because the colleagues English was limited. Of course the colleague was offended. This could have been prevented by further clarifying my intent with the subordinate before sending her off on the mission.

Negotiating between several countries can create even more difficulties. I remember the Korean sales manager at a magazine who had been speaking to a Chinese client in English. He came running into the office elated that he negotiated 12 months worth of advertisements at $3500 each (list price). Later, we discovered the Chinese client had thought it was 12 advertisements for $3500 total. The magazine's president agreed to honor it and the sales manager suffered a severe loss of face. Try to triangulate important points by verifying the response three separate times in different ways. Rephrase the question, asking it in different ways. Remember that misunderstanding can cause hard feelings. Even though you are technically correct, make sure the NP understands well the full meaning.

Avoid absolutes such as always or never, during initial negotiations as they can be confusing and provoke negative reactions. Stick with relative terms that allow a double, face saving interpretation until the basic agreement has been reached. Then continue to clarify until the exact meaning is clearly understood by all sides. Ensure the NP commits to the same agreement you think you made, or as in the example of the sales manager who thought he negotiated 12 advertisements at $3500 each, you may suffer extreme embarrassment.

L. DIFFERENCES IN LANGUAGE

Words are powerful negotiating tools but can be easily misunderstood even by persons who speak the same language. Just imagine how much easier it is for misunderstandings to occur between persons speaking different languages.

Speak slowly to your NP and avoid sounding condescending. This will only offend him and inhibit cooperation.

Assume the NP understands English. Too many executives have been embarrassed because they said something derogatory, thinking the NP could not speak English, only to discover that he comprehends English quite well. On the other hand, don't assume the NP speaks English because he knows a few phrases and says them well. I have heard Americans say it hundreds of times. "That man knows more English than he let's on. He speaks perfectly, he's just playing dumb." It's natural to be suspicious of a persons language ability especially when that person can communicate a few concepts effectively. Both English and Korean are complex and difficult to master. It's easy for me to empathize as I have felt the reverse of this stereotype. Koreans often assume I am fluent, in their language, because I can say certain phrase fairly well, or can speak about certain subjects with confidence. More often than not however, I am almost completely lost if they switch topics to areas other than those with which I have had frequent experience. So please don't suspect, or worse yet accuse, an NP of having more ability than he claims.

At the same time, it is polite to compliment an NP on his English and he may, quite naturally, deny any ability. He is also being polite in his modesty so do not assume he is trying to trick you by being humble. Take the time to write down the promises of an NP. I remember a particular NP with whom I did business frequently. He made promises rather loosely during discussion and later denied them and blamed the misunderstanding on misinterpretations. When I began making notes of his promises he became more careful. He said several times to me, "I must do what I say because you write it down." The problem was effectively eliminated.

The use of idioms is natural for Americans. They are peppered throughout our speech and provide color and distinction to the language. But idioms are frustrating for foreign speakers. They cause confusion and misunderstanding. Idioms conceal

Name	
Football	Tackle the problem, end run, run with the ball, punt, game plan, hit pay dirt, huddle, scramble,
Baseball	Cover all the bases, strike out, never get to first base, 7th inning stretch, out in left field, in the ballpark, a ballpark figure.
Basketball	Slam dunk, fast break, full court press
Wild West	Rein in (Meaning to take control of) Circle the wagons, On the warpath, Chief (Meaning the person in charge), Pow wow, Cowboy (Acting without control. Ex: Joe is out there acting like a cowboy when we need him to follow the rules we developed), Feather in your cap - Meaning a sign of accomplishment. Negotiating that big sale was sure a feather in Bill's cap. Round-up (Meaning to bring together those gone astray), Pan out (Meaning to achieve progress in the end. Ex: The joint venture negotiation just didn't pan out the way we expected), Shoot from the hip.
Railroad	Sidetracked - Strayed from the main objective. Make the grade, End of the line, Railroaded.

other cultural snares that may convey a totally unwanted message. Here is a simple example, the phrase "Don't look back" is meant to show progress and future orientation for Americans, but to historically oriented societies like Korea and China it may communicate a blatant disregard for the past and all it's valuable lessons. The unwary American trying to portray himself as a progressive, forward thinking person, to the NP, may look like a foolish man who does not understand the value of tradition and history.

The main implement in negotiation is language. American English is rich and colorful. Our use of metaphor, analogy, and especially idiomatic phrases leads to creative expression. Idioms in particular, can be difficult to understand for a non-native speaker. When negotiating internationally Americans should avoid idioms to preclude confusion of the issues. Translators also, are not likely to understand what you are trying to convey through idioms, and even if they knew, it would be extremely difficult to translate. By using idioms you will not only exhaust the translator but are likely to create an uncomfortable feeling with your counterpart. A large number of our idioms come from cultural aspects of America not common to Korea. Just for fun, I've included the following idioms derived from our sports and wild-west heritage. A few descriptions are included for the benefit of our foreign readers.

These are just a small sample of the thousands of idioms that were formed as our country aged and are a part of our culture not shared with Korea.

M. STATUS

Good clothes are like the wings of an angel.
"옷이 날개다"
— Korean Proverb

A poorly fed stomach is unseen but a poorly dressed body is readily seen.
"잘입은 거지가 잘 얻어먹는다"
— Korean Proverb

Koreans are alert for status markers. Markers help them pidgin hole you at some level, either above or below them, in the vertical social structure. A short list of important status markers include:

1. Business and home address   2. Clothes & grooming

3. Type of car   4. Official title
5. Schools attended   6. # of Subordinates.
7. Travel experience   8. Contacts

1. While Americans pay less attention to these items they can be of great importance to Koreans. Status can allow you to be perceived as being in a stronger position than you really are and that translates into power that can be advantageous in a negotiation. Americans can appreciate the prestige of a Madison or Park Avenue address but the importance pails in comparison to how Koreans view such matters. Koreans accept living in substandard accommodations and pay outrageous prices just to list an address in the Yong-dong or Apgujeong-dong area of Seoul. Your address in Korea will contribute to your status. If you plan to open an office in Korea, the address should be a consideration.

2. The silent status maker is the clothes you choose to wear. America has become a nation so casual that we sometimes forget other nations practice different traditions. While Korea has adopted a more casual approach in larger companies, clothes are still a distinguishing factor in status. Wear well-made suits and ties and keep them neatly cleaned and pressed. Don't expect the NP to dress casual because it is a weekend. Koreans normally work on Saturdays. Even when attending a social event like a picnic, inquire about the attire. Better to be overdressed that too casual. Take the time to groom yourself as well. It is amazing how many executives neglect to even keep their hair combed and trimmed. Keep your nails manicured and cut.

3. If you maintain an office in Korea or plan to be in Korea for any period of time you will likely purchase a company vehicle. Your vehicle should reflect the status you would like to project or prefer your company to project. Whether to employ a driver may also be a consideration. If your position and status warrants such luxury consider using it. Take a cue from your Korean counterpart.

4. In American companies, titles are often functional and do not become status symbols until the senior executive level. Unfortunately, in their effort to downplay the significance of titles at home American companies suffer when they travel abroad. I remember the American executive who arrived in Korea to negotiate with a large Korean Corporation. His official title, Manager, was high within the structure of his own company. However, within the Korean Corporation he was dealing with, Manager, was a mid-level position of which there were hundreds at that company. The American was shuffled from manager to manager within the Korean company, and was never able to meet the executive level persons he needed to approach. A simple detail such as the proper title on a business card can open the right doors. Give considerable thought as to what title you will carry while abroad.

5. Koreans take great pride in the schools they attended and you should know the differences between alumni of Seoul National University, the premier Korean institution, and other fine schools. Most of the top universities are located in Seoul. Koreans are familiar with the top tier schools in America too. If you are a graduate of an Ivy League school or another top university it is quite acceptable to

mention the name in conversation. Remember, many Korean executives were educated in the US. If by chance you are an alumni of the Korean NP use it to your advantage in establishing a rapport.

6. The number of personnel under your control is not the most prestigious of status markers but is worth mentioning if you are a member of a large company. Size means status in almost any culture. Use it to your advantage if one is to be gained.

7. Travel is an education and your travels may be a way of impressing. Modern Korean executives are well traveled and enjoy discussing their experiences. If you have been to some of the same places it could be a convenient way to generate friendly discussion that might lead to cooperation. Never use your travel experiences to embarrass an NP. If you are well traveled and the NP is not, do not dominate the discussion with your experiences. Mention your travel casually, but let further discussion in that regard be initiated by him.

8. Personal contacts are certainly one of the most important status symbols. If you have, as they say, friends in high places, it is fair game to use them for introductions or mention their names in conversation. Of course it is proper that your contacts agree to allow the use of their name. If you are unfortunate and do not have such contacts, start developing them. This will require a little work and part of your social time but it is indispensable in Korea. Inquire as to the contacts of your employees and friends. With the proper introductions they can become helpful to you. What we call networking in America today was perfected in the Orient centuries ago.

N. LOOK FOR COMMON GROUND

> *Emotion that all the people share.*
> "人之常情(인지상정)"
> — Korean Proverb

Of course, identifying commonalities can help two sides become more cooperative. Focusing on the difference in needs can also help in negotiations when such differences complement each sides goals. It's like the well worn story of the two women arguing how to divide an orange when both needed 3/4 of it. Further discussion revealed one woman was hungry and the other wanted the peels to use in a recipe. By focusing on the common needs (the orange) they could not reach agreement on how to divide it. By focusing on the difference in their needs they could reach agreement more easily (one took the fruit, the other the peels).

O. OFFER ALTERNATIVES

> The more, the better.
> "多多益善(다다익선)"
> — Korean Proverb

Negotiation is really the search for alternatives. Often the solution to a problem is in the alternatives. It may not even involve compromise but just another way of looking at things. For example, I once tore down a small building on my property. The debris consisted of shingles, wood, about 500 cement blocks and window glass. Several contractors estimated it would cost $300 to haul away the debris in four truckloads at $75 a load. I had found a buyer interested in the 500 cement blocks. I originally tried to negotiate $.40 and then $.30 per block but the man would not accept. What he did not have was cash. What he did have was a truck. I agreed to sell the man the blocks for $.25 each or a total cost of $125, if he would haul away a full load of my debris in his truck. He agreed. It did not cost the man anything extra to haul away the debris but it saved me $75. The alternative had effectively raised the value of those blocks to $.40 each although the man actually agreed to pay no more than $.25 per block. It was a win-win solution that was solved by offering an effective alternative.

Price is not the only negotiating point. Include other costs, fees, labor, or services as part of your strategy. Use your imagination in searching for alternatives. In any particular negotiation other factors may be more important than money. Perhaps there is value in the status of an affiliation with a large well-known company. Greater value may be found in the technology transferred, or even in the quality of products or service received. The hidden value may even be in the terms of payment. Find out which alternatives appeal to the needs of the NP.

P. HONOR RITUALS

Picking one's teeth after drinking cold water.
"냉수먹고 이쑤시기"
— Korean Proverb

Throughout a negotiation, you may discover the NP follows rituals or habits, comfortable to him. It may be to your advantage to participate if invited. Even if not invited, it is reasonable to mention a commonality in order to leave open a chance for an invitation. For example, if the NP enjoys discussing matters over breakfast at the Seoul Hyatt Regency, with a morning view of the city, mention that breakfast is your favorite meal. Leave it open for him to offer the invitation. If not, it may still be appropriate to invite him to breakfast.

Rituals appear in a variety of forms. Everything from a trip to the sauna to a drinking party after the close of a deal can be a ritual. While we are on the subject of closing a deal, it is a good idea to close a deal with a drink. Whether you propose a simple toast or schedule an elaborate closing ceremony, be sure and seal the agreement with a word of congratulations. This will generate goodwill and start things off on a positive note.

Situational Negotiations (Examples)

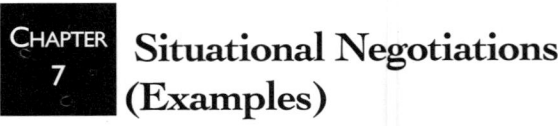

Situational Negotiations (Examples)

CHAPTER 7

A. SHOPPING

Seasoned shoppers know the value of patience. Move slowly in your negotiations. Force the other person to work for every concession. Even before negotiation, sit down with the tailor (or other proprietor), enjoy coffee together, don't be in a rush, ask about his background, his business, his family. Start building a relationship before you ever buy. Show an interest in his work. While you are browsing in Itaewon if a merchant invites you in, accept the invitation and talk with the merchant. Begin building a relationship. Later, when it's time to buy, it will be easier to bargain. In all negotiations you should gather intelligence. In an informal shopping situation gathering intelligence may entail just listening to a merchant deal with other customers before deciding what approach to use with him. But even the smallest bit of information may help you obtain a better deal. Use some of the tips in previous chapters. When shopping try the last minute add on. After negotiating down as low as you feel possible propose the deal clincher it's a deal but you must come down 10% in price. Remember the tactic of Split the difference but always use it as a last resort. Professional shoppers should play reluctant buyer and always find defects in the product as a reason to request a discount. Remember that imaginary defects are still defects. If you want the green sweater and the merchant does not stock a blue one. It is a common negotiating ploy to say you really wanted a blue one but would take the green one at a discount. This form of imaginary defect can be effective with large ticket items as well. Submit the first offer if you are fairly certain of the opponents bargaining range. If a person is selling a jacket for $250 and you are sure it cost him $175, the first offer should be low, maybe $150. This will frame the negotiation and influence him to bargain toward his low end instead of the high end.

B. BUYING ART OR PIECES MADE BY CRAFTSMAN

When negotiating with artists show your appreciation for their work. Then lower the price. Remember, if they have done the work themselves they want to feel appreciated as much as earn a dollar. Explain how you would love to own such a fine piece of craftsmanship but it's a little beyond your price range. Ask the artist to help you own a piece of his work by lowering the price. Explain how you will display it and how many people will see it. If he stands firm on price, try offering a written bid and leave it with him to think over. Include your name and phone number on the bid. Follow-up later to try and convince him to accept your offer. Beware of the rising price tactic. If an artist perceives you are desperate for a particular piece but are firm on the price he may try to raise the price rather than lower it. This sometimes frightens the customer into buying before the price soars even higher. Indicate interest in the artists work but maintain a hint of the reluctant buyer to counter this technique.

C. BUYING / SELLING LARGE TICKET ITEMS

If you are the seller, price the item just above your top figure but below an even number. For example, if your car is worth from

$3500 to $5500 price it at $5900. This will indicate your willing-
ness to bargain. Once again price need not be the only negotiating factor. I once helped negotiate an apartment rental where
the price was a little too high. The owner said we could not
move in until September. We told him we needed to move in by
July 1st. This became a negotiating point we later conceded but
not before negotiating a lower rental fee in return.

When large dollar items are negotiated, you may find yourself at the point where both sides are stuck at a price and will
not move further. I have seen the tactic of flash the money
work quite well. If you have the cash, count it out in front of
the seller, you may be surprised how much influence a large
sum of money exerts when it is actually in front of a person.
Few people will admit it but cold cash can still be quite persuasive.

D. EMPLOYEE / MANAGEMENT NEGOTIATIONS

Most experts would advise to obtain professional help in these
circumstances. However in one-on-one negotiations with
employees remember that as a foreigner you are viewed quite
differently. Sometimes you are perceived as the great benefactor,
the cash cow. Others will imagine you are insensitive to Korean
ways. As a foreigner you will always come out ahead if you
take extra care to show empathy to the Korean employees'
problems. Koreans frequently bring their personal problems to
their boss and ask for help. For example, a young secretary is
taking care of her father and younger brother. She is having
financial difficulty and comes to you looking for help. Be careful
not to turn her away coldly with a reminder that her personal
problems are not the company's problems. Take the time to

show you understand her situation and, at least, offer to try and think of ways that would improve her situation. If employees present a grievance, actually look into it and try to resolve the problem between you. Foster a climate where employees feel confident they will receive fair and honest treatment.

E. NEGOTIATING COMPLAINTS

One of the most difficult situations to negotiate is when you have a complaint and you want satisfaction. Most people approach this situation with so much emotion that they rarely think as clearly as needed and they present the NP an unnecessary advantage. If you are the side with the complaint, spend time preparing for the negotiation just as you would any other situation. First, determine what you want, your money back, an exchange, a replacement, other compensation? Do not become angry, keep a positive attitude while explaining the problem. Don't place blame, ask the NP for help in resolving the complaint. If you are on the other end of the complaint, stay calm, refuse to be affected by their emotionalism. Help the complainant describe the problem and show them you are on their side. Offer solutions and be flexible. When foreigners confront Koreans, the problem suddenly becomes cultural rather than procedural. Don't permit cultural differences become the focus of the complaint. "That stubborn American just doesn't understand how we do things here," or, "that American just doesn't like Koreans," he should never be allowed to become part of a complaint. Keep the emotion out and show empathy and understanding. Be persistent. It may take several tries to succeed.

F. BEWARE OF CURRENCY CONVERSION

When shopping determine if the advantage is to negotiate in won or dollars. For example, you are shopping in Itaewon and the conversion rate is 800 won to $1. As a final offer, the merchant proposes $70, an even figure. It would not be right to offer an odd figure as a counter offer. And the next even figure $60 is too low. Since $70 is (56,000 won) you counter offer 50,000 won, another even figure. Merchants frequently use this tactic to their advantage so why not use it to yours.

Negotiating with Bureaucrats

CHAPTER
8
Negotiating with Bureaucrats

There are private favors even in public affairs.
— Korean Proverb

Negotiating with bureaucrats may seem the toughest of tasks as it appears they have all the leverage. Bureaucrats in general have a reputation of arrogance and aloofness that irritates customers. After all, unlike business administrators if you don't like the service from the government whom can you switch to? You can't! Government bureaucracies may be the worst but large business can present some of the same problems such as slow service and inflexible employees. Americans are familiar with unresponsive bureaucracy and there are hundreds of civil servant and Department of Motor Vehicle jokes to keep the negative stereotype of offensive government alive. But be forewarned that Confucian bureaucracies are in a league by themselves. The attitude of Confucian bureaucracies is founded in a basic cultural difference. In American culture the bureaucracy, at least in theory, serves the public, hence the term civil servant. Americans are not afraid to remind government employees that they work for the taxpayers and at least attempt to hold bureaucrats accountable. In Korea, civil service has enjoyed a long history of honor and status that provided a certain prestige that elevated the civil servant above the citizenry. Grueling tests, required to enter the civil service, demanded years of study and provided an appointee a sense of pride and dignity not equaled in our culture. The Confucian bureaucracy, steeped in tradition, produced dignified civil servants who formed an elite group respected and even feared by common citizens. Even today, Korean civil servants, at times, exhibit a kind of arrogance that may cause a citizen to feel helpless and at their mercy.

Fortunately, there are a few proven methods that will help you get your way. These methods seem to work equally as well in Korea as in America. There are also a few don'ts that can save you unnecessary trouble and actually facilitate a resolution in your favor.

Let's begin with a caution - Never challenge a bureaucrat. Irritated and frustrated customers sometimes vent their anger at bureaucrats only to find themselves in deeper difficulty. The bureaucrats response to anger and emotion is to stiffen in his position and make it impossible for the citizen to win. Remember that the bureaucrat almost always knows the rules better than the citizen does and can surely find a method to foil or further frustrate an unpleasant customer with endless paperwork and delay. On the other hand, making a friend of a bureaucrat can open the doors to your success. A bureaucrat who is inclined to help can permit every loophole, alternative and special waiver, to suddenly become available. Begin making friends by presenting yourself as a person not a problem. Arrive with a positive attitude and maintain it even when matters are not going your way. Prepare yourself before the personal contact. Know exactly what you want and construct a well thought out plan for achieving it before visiting the government office. Initiative or problem solving is not a bureaucrats first reaction to a customer. However, bureaucrats are certainly capable of helping if you gain their interest and cooperation.

Most bureaucrats are spring loaded to fit your situation

within their routine administrative guidelines. Most are reluctant to stray from the routine into areas of risk that might cause them more work or precipitate a controversy. Surprisingly, some bureaucrats can be ignited, to work in your favor by the proper approach. Just asking their opinion may be enough to spark interest. Within their work environment, bureaucrats are not often asked for their opinion even though they have productive ideas. They serve silently, performing the mundane tasks that are uninteresting and under respected by the public. The opportunity to tackle a problem that is out of the ordinary can be intriguing to some bureaucrats. The trick is to approach the right one.

Ask them what they would do in a situation such as yours. Ask for their help, as a person, acknowledge their experience and expertise and enlist their support. Give them a feeling of respect and appreciation and the results can be astonishing. In Korea, it may be helpful to present them a small gift or even invite them to lunch. These methods should be applied carefully and used upon advice from a Korean friend.

Don't speak in bureaucratese. Bureaucrats have a way of making the simplest English or Korean unrecognizable. Consider these two humorous examples and their explanations: "Each canine passes through his period of pre-eminence" or "Every dog has his day." Precipitancy creates prodigality or haste makes waste, and finally "A feathered creature clasped in the manual members" is equal in value to a brace in the bosky bush or more simply stated "A bird in the hand is worth two in the bush." You get the idea. Any idea can be expressed in unnecessarily difficult language. Speak simply and directly to a bureaucrat. It helps to know their jargon but don't try to impress them with it.

Know whom to negotiate with. It is critical that you identify the correct person, in the right section, of the proper department to help you. This may take considerable time if you try to determine it on your own. Bureaucracies are by definition, large, and awkward to navigate. Ask for advice from friends or contacts, even the US Embassy. Networking can save considerable time and money in wasted effort.

In general, bureaucracies are fairly efficient in handling standard cases but far less equipped to deal with unique situations. If you face an unusual circumstance try to persuade the bureaucrat to help you. He may be intrigued by the problem and may put his knowledge to work for you. If this effort is not successful, gage whether it's an individual attitude problem or if the bureaucrat does not possess the authority to deal with exceptions. In either case, go to the person who can help. If possible, persuade the bureaucrat to introduce you to the proper person.

Negotiating may simply involve how a certain rule is applied in your situation. Every public policy contains certain exceptions and loopholes that may be used to your advantage. Loopholes may exist in interpretation of a regulation or the way the current department head enforces certain components of policy. Some call it wiggle room. Loopholes are carefully concealed within a specific policy. The average citizen cannot see past the many shrouds and veils to discover the loopholes, but the bureaucrats can. In negotiating with bureaucrats you should not try to convince them their policy or interpretation is in error, instead try to persuade them to help you exploit the wiggle room necessary to grant your request. A subtle shift in the reading of a rule may change the interpretation in your favor.

Be prepared to put the problem in writing. Bureaucrats are accustomed to dealing with paperwork. Submitting the problem in writing will force dilatory bureaucrats to move along. A letter clearly explaining the problem and the solution can work wonders in attracting the proper attention. Don't just mail the letter as there is too great a risk it will become lost or simply ignored. Present the letter in person and walk it through the process when possible. Prepare several copies in advance.

Be prepared to do their job for them. Bureaucrats appreciate relief from the mundane. If you know certain forms are required to be filled out in advance, prepare them. Don't cause the bureaucrat to feel like you are doing his job because he is incompetent or lazy, present your motivation as appreciating the bureaucrats help and your actions as merely trying to alleviate some of the strain.

We often make the same mistake in Korea and America, that there is one big government and all the separate agencies talk to each other and share all their information. Wrong! Not only don't government agencies always talk to each other they often compete with each other. Be prepared for frustrations between government agencies, but don't complain to bureaucrats about them. Stay positive.

Putting it all together

CHAPTER 9

Putting it all together

Rules for Negotiation

Do	Don't
1. Learn as much as possible about Korea	1. Try to know more than Koreans
2. Try to be culturally sensitive	2. Go native
3. Graciously accept hospitality	3. Be co-opted or influenced by it
4. Rely on locals for advice	4. Abrogate all authority to them
5. Build relationship with Koreans	5. Mistake hospitality for friendship
6. Press your points	6. Cause NP to lose face
7. Be patient	7. Rush or push negotiation too much

Finally, I will recommend the five Ds of negotiation as outlined below.

Rules for Negotiation

Do	Don't
A. Do your Homework	You can't overstate the value of gathering intelligence and background information on your NP.
B. Determine Needs	Find out what the NP really needs and determine if it is possible to satisfy his needs while satisfying your own.
C. Develop Relationships	The relationship is the key to success in Korea.
D. Deal with Obstacles	Find alternatives, seek common ground or do whatever it takes to move forward in the negotiation.
E. Do what you say	Keep your word and protect your reputation. Negotiators live and die by their credibility

Index

Richard Saccone's other books

| TRAVEL KOREA YOUR WAY

Excited about seeing Korea but not sure where to go or what will interest you most? There are scores of places to visit and fascinating things to see, and chances are you don't have time to see them all. This book is designed to provide enough information, about a wide variety of the major attractions, to allow you to piece together the vacation that will suit you best. Just in case it's still to hard to decide, some suggested tours are provided to get you started in the right direction.

216 pages 15.3 x 21 cm full color
ISBN: 1-56591-037-0 (hardcover)
ISBN: 1-56591-012-5 (softcover) LC#: 94-77533

| HAVING A GREAT TOUR: G. I. GUIDE TO KOREA

This book will make your trip to Korea as fun and exciting as it can be. The author toured extensively throughout this country to bring you the most interesting and exciting tourist spots Korea has to offer.
It contains concise information on each location to help you know what to expect from each attraction.
Especially, it includes the maps, photos and information on camps for G. I.

320 pages 15.2 x 21 cm full color softcover
ISBN: 1-56591-067-2 LC#: 96-78392

THE BUSINESS OF KOREAN CULTURE

The modern international business environment demands increased cultural awareness. Everyday, talented businessmen lose money, time, and miss valuable business opportunities because they can't work effectively with their Korean counterparts. The frustration that develops, and the money often lost, is too frequently the result of cultural ineffectiveness. Whether Westerners are on their first trip to Korea or they have visited here for years, chances are they have found working in this wonderful country, at times, as puzzling as it is intriguing. The book is intended to provide background of Korea, and answers to many of those questions, that may have stirred inside foreigners, about working and living in Korea.

200 pages 14 x 21.5 cm b/w illustrations hardcover
ISBN: 1-56591-033-8 LC#: 94-77532

KOREANS TO REMEMBER

While there are many tourists guides and history books that detail famous places in Korea, relatively little is written about the people of Korean history. What little material is available in English is scattered and sometimes difficult to obtain.

To provide an interested reader with the basic details of many historical characters of Korea, the author conducted a survey to choose famous names which Koreans thought foreigners should study if they wanted to develop a basic knowledge of Korea. There are political figures, businessmen religious figures, philosophers, kings, scholars, military figures and artists.

245 pages 14 x 21.5 cm 90 b/w photos hardcover
ISBN: 1-56591-006-0 LC#: 93-77111